"I have made *The Praying Pastor* [...]
grateful for this easy-to-read book [...]
part of one's life and ministry; pray[...]
prayer as the place of learning and g[...], pr[...]
vision; prayer as our most influential moment of the day; and prayer as the place of
intimacy with our heavenly Father."

J. K. Warrick
General Superintendent Emeritus, Church of the Nazarene
Lead Pastor, Parkview Church of the Nazarene
Dayton, Ohio

"Do you know what it's like to sit down with a close friend and talk about something that's important to you? That's what it felt like as I read *The Praying Pastor*. This book is an honest and transparent conversation about prayer. Every pastor understands the temptation to neglect prayer in order to meet the expectations and demands of leadership. When we give in, we suffer great loss. As you read *The Praying Pastor*, you will be gently drawn into the open arms of God, who invites us to know him more."

Rick Harvey
Lead Pastor
Bethany First Church of the Nazarene
Bethany, Oklahoma

"To say that a pastor is an expert in prayer would seem as natural as saying a neurosurgeon knows a thing or two about the human brain! Yet the reality is not as straightforward as it should be. Every pastor *knows* the necessity of a healthy, regular, intimate prayer life, but not every pastor, including myself, always *practices* this. Busyness, multiple tasks and responsibilities, the business of ministry, and even the pastor's own personal and family situation can all creep in and grab time that pushes our needed time with the Lord out. We all know we must prioritize this devotional rhythm, but we don't always manage it. *The Praying Pastor* is just the timely help we need! It is a joy to read. It is profound, personal, practical, and perceptive. I encourage every pastor to read it, for not only is it the work of a seasoned theologian and church leader, but it is also the work of a passionate pastor. A beautiful and honest reflection of Busic's own life as a praying pastor and a man after God's heart."

Jim Ritchie
Eurasia Regional Director
Church of the Nazarene
Büsingen, Germany

"*The Praying Pastor* is a must-read for every pastor who desires to lead with purpose, power, passion, and the perspective of God. Busic's writing is practical and comes from one who lives a life that displays the in-filling power, leadership, and love of Jesus. You will smile as you read about not living like people with our 'hair on fire,' only to then be challenged by the possibilities that emerge for effectiveness, impact, and intercession. Every pastor who wants to lead like Jesus will want to read this book and pass it on to others."

Tim Bunn
Lead Pastor
Eagle Nazarene Church
Eagle, Idaho

"This book is what I was hoping a book about a praying pastor would be. Personal. Pastoral. Practical but not pragmatic. Thoughtful but grounded. It models what it means for prayer to be at the very center of life and ministry. This may be the most important thing Busic has said to the church thus far."

Jeren Rowell
President
Nazarene Theological Seminary
Kansas City, Missouri

"As a pastor, I pray daily for people and situations, at ceremonies and events, over meals and meetings, but am I truly a praying pastor, or just pastor who prays? This deep, necessary, soul-searching question left me needing to know more. I was both challenged and encouraged by Busic's personal and prescriptive words in *The Praying Pastor*. His transparency through his own journey is thought-provoking, reassuring, and transformative as he shares with us practical steps to truly intercede for our families, church leaders, congregants, and others. This book urges all pastors to truly examine our own prayer lives and leaves us better equipped to lead from our knees."

Selena Freeman
Lead Pastor
The Well Church
Springfield, Missouri

"Pastors need help. They are human. Called by God to lead, teach, preach, serve, and love, they often find the challenges of life and ministry overwhelming. *The Praying Pastor* reminds pastors where their help comes from in a manner that moves beyond spiritual clichés. This book is powerfully practical and will be used to help pastors go deeper with God so they can daily live and lead with the guidance and help of the Almighty."

Jeffrey Johnson
South Texas District Superintendent
Church of the Nazarene
Houston, Texas

THE
PRAYING
PASTOR

LEARNING TO LEAD FROM YOUR KNEES

DAVID A. BUSIC

THE FOUNDRY
PUBLISHING

Cover designer: Rob Monacelli
Interior designer: Sharon Page

Library of Congress Cataloging-in-Publication Data
Names: Busic, David A., 1964- author.
Title: The praying pastor : learning to lead from your knees / David A. Busic.
Description: Kansas City, MO : The Foundry Publishing, [2022] | Includes bibliographical references. | Summary: "In the Praying Pastor, David Busic reasons that there's a difference between a pastor who prays and a praying pastor. He examines the vital role of an active and intimate prayer life for every Christian who is called to shepherd Jesus's flock, and urges pastors to move from prayer that feels like an obligation, to that of a desired and necessary activity"— Provided by publisher.
Identifiers: LCCN 2021053034 (print) | LCCN 2021053035 (ebook) | ISBN 9780834141223 | ISBN 9780834141230 (ebook)
Subjects: LCSH: Clergy—Religious life. | Prayer—Christianity.
Classification: LCC BV4011.6 .B87 2022 (print) | LCC BV4011.6 (ebook) | DDC 248.8/92—dc23/eng/20211130
LC record available at https://lccn.loc.gov/2021053034
LC ebook record available at https://lccn.loc.gov/2021053035

10 9 8 7 6 5 4 3 2

◆ ◆ ◆

Dedicated to the praying pastors and chaplains who have served with compassion and courage during the COVID-19 pandemic.

◆ ◆ ◆

If there is any focus that the Christian leader of the future will need, it is the discipline of dwelling in the presence of the One who keeps asking us, "Do you love me? Do you love me? Do you love me?"
—Henri Nouwen

● ● ●

My worth to God publicly is measured by what I really am in my private life.
—Oswald Chambers

CONTENTS

BECOMING A
PRAYING PASTOR

There is a difference between "a pastor who prays" and "a praying pastor." Ponder that statement carefully. At first glance, it may appear to be a minor difference of semantics or a witty wordplay. But I am convinced that the two phrases are dissimilar at best and divergent at worst. They are not the same. The purpose of this book is to demonstrate the distinction in both the phrase and the practice.

Every pastor prays. We pray in worship services, at hospital bedsides, and before committee meetings. We pray at weddings, funerals, and sporting events. We pray over JELL-O salads at church potlucks and over newborn babies in maternity wards. We pray in person, over the phone, and through texts and emails. One could say we are professional pray-ers many times over. It's in our job description. As pastors, we pray.

But being a pastor who prays and being a praying pastor are not the same.[1] A praying pastor engages in more than the ceremonial and the expected. A praying pastor immerses the vocation of pas-

---

1. This is also true for churches. All churches pray, but some are praying churches.

toring—indeed, their entire existence—in the life of prayer. The praying pastor recognizes that prayer is not a duty to perform, a precursor for an action plan, or an add-on blessing to the already decided but that prayer is as essential an act for ministry as oxygen is for breathing. Imagine my surprise, then, when Eugene Peterson, the quintessential teacher of pastors, made the alarming acknowledgment that, "Most pastoral work actually erodes prayer."[2] What could he possibly mean? Certainly, he wasn't referring to the high calling of pastoral ministry and the accompanying time-tested acts of service necessary for shepherding a flock. He is fully aware that the vocational holiness of pastoring requires prayer. Instead, Peterson was describing the expectations—from others and self-imposed—of what it means to be a busy pastor of a growing church.

Few pastors make the conscious decision to be busy at the expense of excluding prayer and eliminating flexibility. It just happens. Calendars fill up without much effort on our part, and if the truth be told, with the exception of Sundays, much of our weekly work can begin to feel strangely secularized. I don't think it is necessary for me to tell pastors how it happens or even why. But we all feel the void when prayer is pushed to the margins. Peterson goes on to say that, when pastors lose their practice of prayer, they soon enter into the habit of being messiah—doing the work of God *for* God, resolving problems, fixing people, and oiling the machinery of church-as-we-have-come-to-expect-it. It is work we are generally good at, indeed, that we have been well trained to do. But this messianic version of pastoring quickly leads to frustrated and exhausted laity and worn down, burned-out pastors. In the words of renowned pastor Earl Lee, "Burnout is the stress and fatigue of the incorrectly committed."

---

2. Eugene H. Peterson, *The Contemplative Pastor: Returning to the Art of Spiritual Direction* (Grand Rapids: William B. Eerdmans Publishing Co., 1989), 43.

I was a lead pastor for three churches over a span of eighteen years. All three churches were healthy and growing. Many people in all three churches were saved, baptized, discipled, sanctified, called into ministry, and engaged in their local communities. They were faithful and fruitful congregations, to the glory of God. And I think I was a good pastor, conscientious and careful, purposeful and disciplined. But if there is one thing I would change if I were to pastor again: I would be a praying pastor.

I certainly went through seasons of being a praying pastor, usually driven by particularly heavy burdens, stressful weeks, or crises too big for me to handle alone. But the rest of the time (which turned out to be most of the time), I prayed generally for God to help me and bless my efforts. I then proceeded to depend on my own giftedness, aptitude, people skills, and intuition to get the job done. I wasn't trying to be disobedient, and I even went through periods when I felt guilty enough about my lack of prayer that I adjusted accordingly (typically starting January 1 or Ash Wednesday). But most of it was temporary and didn't seem to last far beyond the current conflict or refreshed commitment to do better.

I'm not trying to be overly hard on myself. I was growing in my understanding and in my life of prayer. In hindsight, I realize that much of my prayer life as a pastor was dependent on what I could and could not control. The truth is, as a lead pastor, in most circumstances I could alter the trajectory of a congregation in a few months. I could preach sermons, cast vision, raise funds, call meetings, and have any number of meetings and conversations with influencers. I had access to key leaders and relational capital to spend. The subtle irony is that, when I had greater control, I prayed less.

Now I am a general superintendent in my denomination, and there are more than two million members who don't know me. I am an ecclesial authority at best, a figurehead at worst. I have far less control over outcomes than I ever did as the pastor of a local church. But it's not a bad thing. With less control, I am becoming a praying

A praying pastor immerses the vocation of pastoring—indeed, their entire existence—

in the life of prayer.

general superintendent. I no longer merely pray for God to bless my decisions, and then move ahead as I see fit. With less control, I feel a greater need to bathe every decision in prayer, to keep company with God, to linger in the Lord's presence without the need to fill up the air with my words, to soak in the world of Scripture, to process knowledge with discernment, and to grow deeper in my understanding and practice of intercession. In short, I am learning to lead from my knees. The upshot is not more control but greater surrender. Not more power but greater peace. Not greater determination but greater dependence with a more restful heart—and potentially, by God's grace, more lasting fruit.

One of the tricks of life is that we don't know what we could have had; we only know what we actually have. What *would* have and *could* have been different if I had been more committed to intercessory prayer as a lead pastor? Would there have been different outcomes? More enduring fruit? A more impactful harvest? I don't have many regrets from my pastoral ministry. God gave great grace, and I believe I was a good pastor. But I wish I had put more emphasis on the life of prayer and less dependence on my natural instincts, abilities, and strengths.

In rereading the classic Bible verse on slowing down, "Be still and know that I am God" (Psalm 46:10), I discovered that the Latin imperative for "be still" is *vacate*. In a play on words, Simon Tugwell offers a fresh paraphrase of this verse from Psalm 46: "God invites us to take a holiday, to stop being God for a while, and let him be God."[3] Take a vacation from being God! Take a break from trying to make things happen in your own strength, and rely on God's strength instead. Those commands (and they *are* commands) are jet fuel for the praying pastor. *There is a God, and it is not me.*

---

3. Simon Tugwell, *Prayer: Living with God* (Springfield, IL: Templegate Publishers, 1975), 35.

I am still growing in my understanding and practice of prayer. The explicit goal of a book like this is not to create guilt over a failure to pray, or to plant an impetus to continue in the same generalized petitions we may have been praying up to this point. This book is not a how-to manual, although I hope you will find help from my own journey with prayer. My promise to you is that I will endeavor to make this book a guilt-free zone. Some laity hear an announcement about next week's sermon on prayer and mentally buckle their seatbelts for the collision they know is coming. If there is a collision coming for you, let it be from the Holy Spirit and not from me. I hope to encourage you toward a growing desire to pray; toward an increased, intentional practice of prayer; to take a vacation from being God and renew the conviction that "a life of prayer is the connective tissue between holy day proclamation and weekday discipleship."[4]

One last thing before we dive into the deep end. We call prayer a "practice," and rightly so. As a spiritual discipline, it is. But as you read this book, I hope it will also become clear to you that prayer is not just a practice—it is the game.

---

4. Peterson, *The Contemplative Pastor*, 59.

WHAT IS PRAYER?

Someone once asked Mother Teresa the secret of her ministry. I am struck by her unpretentiousness: "My secret is a very simple one: I pray." The follow-up question, "What is prayer?" yielded another uncomplicated yet profound response: "Prayer is simply talking to God. He speaks to us: we listen. We speak to him: he listens. A two-way process: speaking and listening."[1]

There are many definitions of prayer, and no doubt, each one emphasizes a particular aspect of prayer that is important to understand. But, at its most fundamental level, prayer is communication. It is us speaking to God and God listening. And it is God speaking to us and us listening. Though not equal partners, it is a conversation between two persons who, by the grace of God, mutually contribute to the dialogue.

According to Eugene Peterson, the biblical psalms are arranged in such a way as to protect us from presumptuous prayer that speaks to God without first listening. Many people (pastors included) are in the habit of talking *about* God, not *to* God. But, as Peterson points

---

1. Mother Teresa and Anthony Stern, *Everything Starts from Prayer: Mother Teresa's Meditations on Spiritual Life for People of All Faiths* (Ashland, OR: White Cloud Press, 1998), 35.

out, the book of prayer we call Psalms is provided to help us resist this temptation. They teach us that God always speaks first, always has the first word (33:9). Moreover, the psalms are given not only to teach us about God but also to train us in responding to him.[2] In other words, we are not in charge of prayer.

Prayer, in its most basic form, starts with an act of listening, of paying attention to Spirit-prompted conversation and responding through our words and actions. When we do all the talking, we minimize the ultimate purpose and benefit of prayer. Prayer is not a monologue—it is dialogue grounded in a covenantal relationship. We are, by design, creatures made for conversation: "We humans represent the only species on earth [who] . . . can form words in response to the miracle, and also the tragedy, of life. We dare not devalue this unique role in the cosmos, to give words to existence, words addressed to our Creator. God eagerly bends an ear toward those words."[3]

The blueprint for prayer is not complicated: God speaks—we listen; we speak—God listens. Holy conversation. Can it be that straightforward? Is that why a child's naïve yet trusting prayer for a pet matters as much to God as a seasoned saint's prayer of intercession? Let's dig a little deeper.

Knowing God

The goal of all good communication is to know and to be known by the person with whom one is communicating. Thus, prayer in its highest form is rooted in a relationship with the goal of knowing God and of God knowing us. There are many references to prayer in the

---

2. Eugene H. Peterson, *As Kingfishers Catch Fire: A Conversation on the Ways of God Formed by the Words of God* (Colorado Springs, CO: Waterbrook, 2017), 60–61.

3. Philip Yancey, *Prayer: Does It Make Any Difference?* (Grand Rapids: Zondervan, 2006), 43.

Bible, many of which we will consider. But for me, one of the most important texts on prayer doesn't even mention the word.

The value of reading from multiple Bible translations is that nuances are revealed that we might miss if we only read from a single translation. Various textual vantage points provide a better understanding of the original language's intended meaning. Three different translations of Proverbs 3:5–6 demonstrate this point.

> Trust in the LORD with all your heart and lean not on your own understanding; in all your ways **submit** to him, and he will make your paths straight (emphasis added).

> Trust in the LORD with all your heart, and do not rely on your own insight. In all your ways **acknowledge** him, and he will make your paths straight (NRSV, emphasis added).

> Trust in *and* rely confidently on the LORD with all your heart And do not rely on your own insight *or* understanding. In all your ways **know** *and* **acknowledge** *and* **recognize** him, and he will make your paths straight *and* smooth [removing obstacles that block your way] (AMP, bold added, italics original, brackets original).

These translations are mostly the same, except for one word that biblical scholars and translators can't seem to fully agree on. The elusive word is *yâda'* (pronounced *yaw-DAH'*), which means "to know." It is a common Hebrew word used many times throughout the Old Testament.[4] It can mean "to know," "to know by experience," or "to perceive." In the Christian sense, it is knowing as firsthand, personal knowledge—particularly, knowing another person.

Of most interest for the language of prayer, *yâda'* is also the standard reference for sexual intimacy between a husband and wife (for

---

4. Strong's Hebrew Concordance in the NASB indicates that the word occurs 1,007 times in 872 verses.

example, Adam *yâda'* Eve, and Cain was born). It is noteworthy that Song of Solomon (also referred to as Song of Songs) is located in the Wisdom section of the Bible—specifically in the prayer section of the Hebrew Scriptures alongside Psalms. We often read it through our modern lens as a book about human love—a love story between a man and woman. The original composer of Song of Solomon believed it to be a love story as well—but between God and the person in prayer.

Reading the book in this metaphorical way gives renewed meaning to the romance of prayer and an illuminating insight into the ultimate reason we pray. We do not pray because it is the way to get something from God—or, for that matter, even to discover the will of God. The goal of prayer is not to work through our list of requests, hoping to prod God to act. Instead, the purpose of prayer is to *know* God, personally and intimately. A personal prayer mentor of mine says it well: "Prayer is not getting things from God, that is a most initial stage; prayer is getting into perfect communion with God."[5]

Looking at prayer this way debunks the prevalent idea that God's will is a covert plan dropped from the sky and that Christians are code breakers whose job is to connect the dotted lines. In some ways this might be easier. A map is more tangible than a relationship. But it is not the way we discover God's plans. We learn God's plans as we learn to know God. There is a reason God has designed it in this way. If we seek plans, then we will focus on the plans instead of on Jesus. "We would begin to build our lives around God's purposes for us instead of around God himself."[6] This is also the reason Jesus told us to follow him instead of a moral code. He is not the tour guide on the way—he *is* the way. The distinction is subtle,

---

5. Oswald Chambers, *Studies in the Sermon on the Mount: God's Character and the Believer's Conduct* (Grand Rapids: Discovery House Publishers, 1995), 51.

6. Dennis F. Kinlaw with Christiane A. Albertson, *This Day with the Master: 365 Daily Meditations* (Grand Rapids: Zondervan, 2002), 146.

At its most fundamental level, prayer is us speaking to God and God listening and God speaking to us and us listening.

but it is ultimately the difference between religion and relationship. We need *Jesus* more than anything we might get *from* Jesus. Dennis Kinlaw accurately writes, "The life that does not arise out of a personal, intimate knowledge of Jesus will ultimately, no matter how good, be frustrating, sterile, and unfulfilling. But the life that is lived in the immediacy of daily, hourly, continual contact with him will be fruitful and joyous."[7]

The goal of prayer is to know—*yâda'*—God. This relational dynamic is what keeps prayer from becoming monotonous, perfunctory, and boring.

Why Prayer Matters

To pray is to give attention to our most vital relationship. It is giving prioritized time to align our hearts to God's heart. I like Clement of Alexandria's definition of prayer: "Prayer is keeping company with God."[8]

Former Archbishop of Canterbury Rowan Williams lightheartedly suggests that prayer is putting yourself where *God can get at you*. When asked by an interviewer why someone should pray if God is present throughout the day to help us anyway, the Archbishop paused and then said with a twinkle in his eye, "When you're on holiday with the family, they're with you all day. You're aware of it. But it would be a very bad family holiday if you didn't sometimes just sit down across the table with children or spouse and say, 'Here we are. Let's enjoy the moment'—not just running around. And I think that's part of where prayer fits in. It's the sitting across the table and saying [to God], 'Well, here we are. Let's enjoy this moment together.'"[9]

---

7. Kinlaw, *This Day with the Master*, 146.

8. Clement of Alexandria, quoted in Tugwell, *Prayer*, 35.

9. Rowan Williams, interview with Aled Jones for *Songs of Praise*, 2010, https://www.youtube.com/watch?v=S1RvKQU78zQ.

Creator to creation—Person to person—Friend to friend—Father to child—Beloved to beloved. Prayer is about coming to know God. But there is more. As we come to know God, we also come to know ourselves. When we pray, we realize we're not talking to ourselves in some kind of inner dialogue. The Spirit of God is praying within us, communicating the will of the Father and laying bare the deepest secrets of our hearts. In truth, prayer may be the only reliable entryway into genuine self-knowing.

Flannery O'Connor, the famous Southern writer of several classics, was only twenty-one when she began keeping a prayer journal. As a Christian, she learned to pray her feelings through writing them down. Tim Keller reflects on his study of her journey with prayer: "O'Connor learned that prayer is not simply the solitary exploration of your own subjectivity. You are with Another, and he is unique. God is the only person from whom you can hide nothing. Before him, you will unavoidably come to see yourself in a new, unique light."[10]

Self-realization, or self-actualization, is a popular type of spirituality today. A quick Google search of "how to get in touch with my inner self" yielded 683,000,000 results in 0.64 seconds. Scanning a few of these sites, I was encouraged to spend time in nature, schedule solo dates, take yoga classes, meditate, travel, take long walks, and keep a soul journal. But here's the problem: religions that invite me to get in touch with my true self without being centered on God will never succeed because the only voice speaking is my own—a perpetual echo chamber. Christian prayer, on the other hand, offers me the possibility of actually hearing from Another who is not me but who knows me. "Prayer," Keller concludes, "leads to a self-knowledge that is impossible to achieve any other way."[11]

---

10. Timothy Keller, *Prayer: Experiencing Awe and Intimacy with God* (New York: Penguin Books, 2014), 12.

11. Keller, *Prayer*, 12.

There is a difference between knowledge and knowing. Few people have expressed the difference more poignantly than C. S. Lewis. For me, his writings on pain, joy, and prayer are unsurpassed in distinguishing the thin space between knowing God and knowing oneself. Lewis maintains that we are completely known by God—not just known as *things*, like God has knowledge of "earthworms, cabbages, and nebulae," but known as *persons*. In that sense, being known completely by God "is our destiny whether we like it or not. But though this knowledge never varies, the *quality* of our being known can."[12] Therefore, Lewis contends, the prayer preceding all prayers should be, "May it be the real I who speaks. May it be the real thou that I speak to."[13] Only in this way will our prayers preserve the proper order of adjusting ourselves to God than adjusting God to ourselves.

During an extended period of personal theodicy, when Lewis strained under the burden of God's seeming silence in the face of heartrending tragedy, he came to this conclusion: "I know now, Lord, why you utter no answer. You are yourself the answer. Before your face questions die away. What other answer would suffice?"[14]

When we come face to face with God, we are confronted with what is most true about us and about the way we experience deep change. Like Moses's encounter in the wilderness, this is the holy ground where the bush of God's glory burns with most radiant brilliance. What issues from that is what Glaphré—my intercessory prayer partner—taught me is the follow-up process to complete commitment: a life of dependency framed in a disciplined pursuit of intimacy with God. This disciplined dependency will require al-

---

12. Clive Staples Lewis, *Letters to Malcolm: Chiefly on Prayer* (London: Geoffrey Bles, 1964), 20, emphasis added.

13. Lewis, *Letters to Malcolm*, 109.

14. Lewis, *Till We Have Faces: A Myth Retold* (New York: HarperCollins, 1984), 351.

ways consulting with God instead of relying on our own ideas and decisions.[15] It is a resolve that is renewed with each new moment, each new event, and each new need to abandon independent thinking and finally treat God as God. It is to let him direct each moment in lieu of my frenetic efforts to justify my ministry by hyperactively doing things instead of waiting on God to lead. In short, it is to be a praying pastor even when it "seems to be a distraction from so much that needs doing."[16]

Becoming a Praying Pastor

As we explore aspects of what it means to be a praying pastor in the chapters ahead, let us keep this thought foremost in our minds: the goal of prayer is to know God. When praying pastors pray for vision, we ask God to help us see things like he does—including ourselves.

15. Glaphré Gilliland, *When the Pieces Don't Fit: God Makes the Difference* (Bethany, OK: Prayerlife Ministries, 1984), 125–26.

16. Richard John Neuhaus, *Freedom for Ministry* (Grand Rapids: William B. Eerdmans Publishing Co., 1992), 137.

WHAT JESUS SAID ABOUT PRAYER

I am not an expert on prayer. Even as I write this sentence, I am keenly aware of how far I have to go in my understanding and practice of prayer. There are many moments when I feel as if I'm still in prayer kindergarten. Are pastors allowed to say things like this? How can we teach others to pray when it can feel like such a struggle for the ordained?

I had the privilege of growing up in a praying home. My parents were not pastors, but they set an example of prayer for my younger sister and me. Some of my earliest memories are of our family gathering to pray in the living room. My sister and I sat on the couch, and someone would read a story from our family Bible. Then we all knelt and took time to pray for various things, including our pastor, the people of our church, and missionaries in the denominational missions magazine. Then we prayed for extended family—aunts and uncles and some cousins I had never met. More often than not, I fell asleep during prayer time and miraculously woke up the next morning in my bed. These were not the most exhilarating moments of my childhood, but I knew prayer must be important if my mom and dad were willing to make it a rule of life. A prayer practice was ingrained into my imagination.

As I became older, I remember waking up every morning around seven. I had an alarm clock, but I usually didn't need it because my dad would wake me with his praying. My room was in the rear of the house, attached to our small kitchen. There my dad would sit at a little dinette table and have his quiet time with the Lord. He didn't pray loudly, but he prayed out loud. While I didn't fully appreciate it then, hearing my father pray specifically for me on a daily basis had an impact on a teenage son who was trying to find his way.

So when I began to think seriously about my own spiritual journey, it seemed natural to assume that prayer was something I also needed to do. I vowed to get up early every morning and pray for an hour, just like my dad. My first attempt did not go as planned. I was nineteen, married, going to school full-time, and working nearly full-time. I got up at five o'clock in the morning to have time to pray. I prayed for everyone I could think of: relatives, neighbors, people at church. I prayed for various countries of the world. I prayed for missionaries. I prayed for hungry people. I prayed for the president. I prayed for every person and everything I could think of. Then I glanced at the clock to make sure I hadn't gone over the allotted hour—I had prayed for twelve minutes. I gutted it out and prayed for the full hour (not counting the times I went to the sink to throw water on my face). It felt good to persevere in prayer, but I couldn't help but wonder if this was what prayer was really all about and if this was a habit I could maintain.

I tried again the next morning and the morning after that. But praying like this became harder and harder, and it wasn't long before I stopped. I was frustrated. I felt guilty (guilt has always been one of my spiritual gifts). I knew I needed to be praying better than I was. I knew it was a vital part of my walk with Christ, but I couldn't will myself to be more consistent. For all the reasons I knew I should be praying, I didn't seem to have the willpower to do it. Praying felt more like labor than joy. I was defeated about the very thing I knew should give me strength.

It wasn't that I *never* prayed. I continued to pray for a few minutes during my daily quiet time with God, I prayed before meals, and I found the energy to pray earnestly when I was desperate. Every New Year, I pushed the reset button on my personal spiritual goals and vowed to do better, but it wasn't very satisfying. Deep in my spirit, I believed there was a better way to pray. I hoped there was something more.

So I began to study prayer. I became interested in finding out how the great pray-ers of the Bible prayed: Abraham, Moses, Elijah, Hannah, David, Hezekiah, Hosea, Daniel. How did they pray? When did they pray? What did they pray? Most importantly, I studied the prayer life of Jesus. I read of how often he got away from the crowds to be alone with his Father. I read about times he prayed *all* night long and contemplated: *What could he possibly have to pray about for the entire night?* I read about how he taught his disciples to pray. I read about the prayer he prayed for all his followers, then and now. I read about how he spent his last night praying in a garden with such intensity that his sweat turned to blood. And I read about how he prayed for his enemies as he died on the cross, and how even his final breath was a prayer. It became apparent to me that prayer wasn't just a routine for Jesus—it was like breathing. Jesus must have known something about prayer that I had yet to discover. I wanted to know more. I wanted to experience what Jesus said is true:

And when you pray, do not be like the hypocrites, for they love to pray standing in the synagogues and on the street corners to be seen by others. Truly I tell you, they have received their reward in full. But when you pray, go into your room, close the door and pray to your Father, who is unseen. Then your Father, who sees what is done in secret, will reward you. And when you pray, do not keep on babbling like pagans, for they think they will be heard because of their many words. Do not be like them, for your Father knows what you need before you ask him. (Matthew 6:5–13)

The context of Jesus's teaching on prayer is the Sermon on the Mount. Importantly, the sermon is directed to disciples, not to crowds. Jesus begins with *"when* you pray," assuming, first, that his disciples *will* pray, and second, that there are other notions of prayer besides the one Jesus lays out for us. We will deal with Jesus's concept of "praying in secret" in another chapter. I want to look first at his second point, the difference between pagan prayer and Christian prayer.

"Pagan" (*ethnikoi*) is an interesting concept, by which Jesus was referring to the large constituent of people who were neither Jewish nor Christ followers.[1] Instead, their religious preferences derived from the pantheon of Greek gods, of whom there were literally dozens to choose from. Jesus specifically addresses the nature of pagan prayer. "And when you pray, do not keep on babbling like pagans, for they think they will be heard because of their many words." The word translated "babbling" (*battalogesete*) can mean "vain or meaningless repetitions" or, as the NRSV puts it, "to heap up empty phrases"—in other words, piling one prayer on top of another. Pagan prayer rested on the conviction that the gods didn't want to hear their prayers to begin with. Therefore, their prayer plan had two parts.

Pagan prayer strategy #1: Tell the gods what they want to hear. Appease the gods. Feed their egos so they will be more inclined to listen. This mentality was so deeply ingrained that many began to think knowing the name of a particular god and pronounc-

---

1. The NIV uses the word "pagan" instead of "gentile." *Ethnikos* can mean "gentile," "heathen," or "pagan." It generally refers to a non-covenant person in relationship to God. Jesus's usage here seems to be less about people from non-Israel nations and more about a specific spiritual connotation.

ing it correctly in an incantation gave them magical power to manipulate a god to give them what they asked.

Pagan prayer strategy #2: Exhaust the gods. Bombard the gods with such a barrage of words that they will grow tired of listening and give you almost anything to make you shut up. There was actually a prayer ploy in the Greek world termed "fatigue the gods." The rationale was simple. Because the gods were self-serving, unpredictable, and didn't want to hear prayers anyway, the best thing one could do was pound them with so many words that it would eventually wear them out.

Muhammed Ali was arguably the greatest heavyweight boxer of all time. Early in his career, his self-proclaimed fighting style was to "float like a butterfly, sting like a bee." As he aged, he developed a new technique called the "rope-a-dope," where he would spend the first several rounds defensively covered up in the corner of the boxing ring while his opponent pounded his protected head and body with ineffective punches. The objective was to wear down his challenger so that, when Ali went on the offensive, they were too tired to fight back. Pagan prayer was kind of like the rope-a-dope. Except the gods were the ones on the ropes, being pounded by requests and complaints until they were finally so frustrated or worn out that they finally threw up their hands and exclaimed: "Enough already! I'll give you whatever you want—just stop bugging me and leave me alone!" Hence the word "babble," or "piling up empty phrases"—pouring it on thick.[2]

A prime example of pagan prayer is found in 1 Kings 18:16–40. Elijah, the prophet of God, challenges the prophets of Baal and Asherah (foreign gods) to a showdown that will determine whose deity is

---

2. Babble as a verb can mean "to prattle, utter words indistinctly, or to talk like a baby." The Greek word *barbaros*, meaning "non-Greek speaking," eventually became associated with the concept of barbarians—those of inarticulate and idle speech.

more powerful. It is four hundred fifty prophets of Baal and four hundred prophets of Asherah versus the one prophet of Israel's God, Elijah: 850 to 1. The idea is to see whose deity will consume the sacrifice.

The prophets of Baal and Asherah go first. They slaughter a bull and place it on the altar. Then they begin praying to their gods. They fervently pray for hours, from morning until noon, but there is no response. Accordingly, they start dancing around the sacrifice and working themselves into a frenzy, still to no avail.

Elijah does not hesitate to taunt them: "Are your gods hard of hearing? Perhaps if you yell a little louder they could hear you! Are they taking a nap? Are they on vacation?" This is the ancient equivalent of trash-talking. Elijah's provocation induces the prophets to increase their intensity. They resort to cutting themselves until they are covered with blood and sweat. Surely their gods will see their commitment and take them seriously. They carry on like this all day with no divine response.

When it is Elijah's turn, he asks for water to be poured onto the sacrifice so that no one will assume that the Baal and Asherah prophets' efforts preheated things. Then Elijah prays two sentences, and fire flashes from heaven, completely consuming the sacrifice, the altar, and even the excess water that puddled in the trench around the altar.

The disparity is striking. The pagans "babble," as it were, all day long, dancing frenetically, frothing at the mouth, mutilating their bodies—but receive no divine response. This is pagan prayer in brief. Elijah said a few simple words, and God sent fire from heaven.

By playfully retelling the story of Elijah on Mount Carmel, the essential condition of pagan prayer is exposed: unless a prayer is long and filled with many words, the gods won't listen; and if they do listen, it will only be after the pray-er has proven to be serious, piling on the compliments, stroking the god's ego, and telling them what they want to hear. It sounds outlandish in theory and uncivilized to modern ears, but consider how Christians sometimes approach prayer. Do we believe that, the harder we work at prayer, the better prayer is? Do we suppose that God is more persuaded to respond to an hour of prayer than one sentence? If so, why? Is God impressed by our eloquence? Is God more inclined to answer the prayers that are most earnestly expressed or that say what God wants to hear?

Whether these notions of prayer are explicit beliefs or implicit practices, they serve to project God as an ogre who begrudgingly gives, who can be manipulated and bargained with if we play it just right. God is the petulant monarch to whom we play court jester; God is the organ grinder, and we are the lackey capuchin monkeys turning tricks for his attention. But that is nothing more than a subtly repackaged form of pagan prayer, and Jesus unabashedly calls it out as misguided.

Eugene Peterson's paraphrase of Jesus's response is enlightening: "The world is full of so-called prayer warriors who are prayer-ignorant. They're full of formulas and programs and advice, peddling techniques for getting what you want from God. Don't fall for that nonsense. This is your Father you are dealing with, and he knows better than you what you need. With a God like this loving you, you can pray very simply" (Matthew 6:7–8, MSG).

Jesus's Parables about Prayer

The evangelist known as Luke, and the only New Testament writer who is clearly identifiable as a non-Jew, frames Jesus's teaching on prayer in the context of parables. The first of these parables, found in Luke 11:5–8, is called by various names, perhaps most commonly "the friend at midnight." The context of the story is first-century village life, particularly highlighting ordinary peasants who survived by the hospitality of their neighbors. There were few, if any, shops in the average Galilee village, and most of the baking and other food preparation was done by families in their homes. These homes were modest, one-room dwellings where parents and children all slept in the same area.

We don't have to harangue God, impress God, or stroke God's ego to get him to listen to our prayers.

Jesus invites his hearers to imagine a scenario where a traveler arrives at a Jewish home unexpectedly during the night. The host is obligated to feed the unexpected guests, but to his dismay, he realizes there is not enough on hand to offer an adequate meal. Out of a sense of honor to meet the demands of Middle Eastern hospitality, the host slips into the night and, going from house to house, gathers the needed ingredients. This is not an exceptional act of kindness—it is expected. This is why Jesus begins by saying, "Suppose one of you," an expression that literally means, "Which one of you?" with the rhetorical answer being, "None of you." Any good Jewish neighbor would do whatever is necessary to meet the need. So he goes to a friend's home to ask for bread, the basic subsistence of a meal. He does not ask for lamb (he knows what time it was). He asks for what is most probably available at that hour.

The neighbor is already in bed and doesn't even bother to rise. He supposedly answers without getting up (most likely in a hushed tone), "Don't bother me. The door is already locked, and my children and I are in bed. I can't get up and give you anything" (Luke 11:7). This is an unwelcome and badly timed request. It is night. The door is locked. The kids are finally asleep, and now this interruption. But the awakened man eventually gets up and grants his neighbor's request. Why? This is where translators and preachers differ in their exegesis. Where is the emphasis? Is it on the action of the seeking host or of the sleeping neighbor?

If one emphasizes the seeking host, then the translation might be that the sleeping neighbor eventually gets up to help because of the seeking host's "shameless audacity" (NIV), or because of the host's "persistence" (NRSV). While both are positive actions, they are clearly not the same—just as courage and perseverance are not identical. Nevertheless, the focus in this view is on the action of the seeking host.

However, the other way to translate it is to emphasize the action of the sleeping neighbor, who does not respond out of friendship but because he knows that communal hospitality is his duty even if the guests are not in his own home. The linguistic pivot for the meaning of the parable is *anaideia*, which means "shamelessness," as in "lacking shame" or "behaving shamelessly."[3] When asked in question form, the phrase is one we are familiar with: "Have you no shame?" The classic Jewish historian of the first century, Josephus, always uses the word *anaideia* in this way, causing some translators of Josephus to use the word "impudent."[4] This is very interesting. If this is the more accurate translation of *anaideia*, who is the shameless one in Jesus's story?

Grammatically, the antecedent of both "his friend" and "his shamelessness" is not the seeking host but the sleeping neighbor.[5] Said differently, the sleeping neighbor does not act out of a sense of honor, friendship, and mutual obligation but only out of the avoidance of shame, afraid he will be disgraced in the community if it is discovered that he failed to act with hospitality. Bernard Brandon Scott summarizes it well: "[The sleeping neighbor] has done out of shamelessness what he ought to have done out of honor."[6] If he acts on behalf of his seeking friend, it would be honorable. But because he acts only to protect his reputation in the community, then he acts primarily out of self-interest and is shameless.

This is a different way to understand the meaning of the parable, and it becomes problematic, especially if one correlates the seeking host with the praying Christian and the sleeping neighbor as God (as many people do). Certainly, it cannot mean that the one

3. G. W. H. Lampe, *A Patristic Greek Lexicon* (Oxford: Clarendon, 1961), 103.

4. Josephus, *Jewish Antiquities*, trans. and ed. Ralph Marcus, ed. Allen Wikgren (Cambridge: Harvard University Press, 1963), 427.

5. Kenneth E. Bailey, *Poet and Peasant: A Literary-Cultural Approach to the Parables in Luke* (Grand Rapids: William B. Eerdmans Publishing Co., 1976), 128.

6. Bernard Brandon Scott, *Hear Then the Parable: A Commentary on the Parables of Jesus* (Minneapolis: Fortress Press, 1989), 91.

who prays should shamelessly bring their requests to God. Likewise, it cannot mean that God is more likely to respond to prayers due to our persistence—or worse, that God answers prayers based on the self-serving purpose that he will be disgraced by the perception of his indifference.[7] So what, exactly, *is* Jesus trying to say about prayer? More importantly, what is he saying about God?

Before we come to that answer, let's consider another parable that Jesus tells about prayer in Luke 18. "Then Jesus told them a parable about their need to pray always and not to lose heart" (v. 1, NRSV). "Them," according to 17:22, is assumed to be the disciples, and the purpose of the parable, according to Luke, is clearly to illustrate the nature of perseverance in prayer.

Jesus begins the story by identifying a certain judge in a certain city. The judge is characterized by a lack of shame—he does not fear God or respect people. This description offers a not so subtle implication about the judge's moral integrity. Though a fear of God and a respect for people seem to be important qualities for someone expected to administer justice, it was not uncommon for first-century judges to be corrupt. He is an immoral judge with concerns only for his own self-interest. Nothing shames him. He possesses no honor to which one can appeal for justice. Not even a destitute widow who has run out of options can move him to empathy. His internal compass of right and wrong is askew. His conscience has been seared by too many bribes and, perhaps, compassion fatigue.

The next person to enter the parable is the widow. The biblical perspective of the widow is a vivid symbol of the powerless and oppressed. The Hebrew prophets' calls for purity are always twofold:

---

7. Kenneth Bailey makes a strong case that, in order to make sense of this parable, the church felt the necessity of taking the negative quality of "shamelessness" and turning it into the positive quality of "persistence." The change of meaning in most Bible translations was complete by the twelfth century. Bailey, *Poet and Peasant*, 126–27.

stop doing evil things, and start doing righteous things.[8] Avoiding evil is only part of the equation. The people must also learn to act justly. And justice always starts with the most vulnerable and dispossessed—namely, "Cease to do evil, learn to do good; seek justice, rescue the oppressed, defend the orphan, plead for the widow" (Isaiah 1:16b–17, NRSV). "Pleading for the widow" is a phrase that has legal connotations of a lawyer arguing on behalf of a voiceless person in a court. Based on these admonitions, the Jewish legal system required a specific order for how all cases must be heard: "The suit of an orphan must always be heard first; next, that of a widow . . ."[9] This was the judicial order because of the level of powerlessness. Orphans and widows had no one to protect them. Thus, judges were required by God to give special and priority consideration to their cases.

The widow in Jesus's example is coming to the judge because someone is withholding something of monetary value from her—perhaps a portion of her inheritance or an unpaid debt. Her deceased husband cannot advocate for her, and apparently no one in her extended family can either. So, at considerable risk, she comes to the only one who has the power to act on her behalf.[10] She is not asking for retribution, only for what is rightfully hers. But the judge ignores her. His heart has been hardened by too many widows with sob stories, and this one has no money to slip him under the table. She is helpless to do anything except persevere.

---

8. John Wesley picks up on this prophetic theme in his General Rules for Methodist societies: "Do no harm; do good."

9. L. N. Dembitz, "Procedure in Civil Causes" in *The Jewish Encyclopedia: Volume X, Philipson–Samoscz* (New York: Funk and Wagnalls, 1905), 102–106. Cited in Kenneth E. Bailey, *Through Peasant Eyes: More Lukan Parables, Their Culture and Style* (Grand Rapids: William B. Eerdmans Publishing Co., 1980), 133.

10. "Ordinarily women in the Middle East did not go to court. The Middle East was and is a man's world, and women are not expected to participate with men in the pushing, shouting world [of the ancient court system, in which cases would be called from clamoring crowds]." Bailey, *Through Peasant Eyes*, 134.

At first, the judge is recalcitrant. Perhaps the widow's adversary has more to offer him than she does. Whatever the reason, he refuses to help her. Then, seemingly out of the blue, the judge experiences an "aha!" moment and follows it up with a self-talk. "Though I have no fear of God and no respect for anyone, yet because this widow keeps bothering me, I will grant her justice, so that she may not wear me out by continually coming" (18:4b–5, NRSV). He is self-aware enough to know that his morality won't be the deciding factor in rendering the verdict, but he also knows that the widow is determined to have justice.

The word that is translated "wear me out" is a boxing term that means to give someone a black eye.[11] The context of his words makes clear that the judge isn't worried that the widow will become violent but that she will be relentless.[12] The Arabic translation of the verse, "Lest she give me a headache," is a metaphorical way to express the extent to which her persistence is irritating him.[13] Further, the Greek phrase that is translated "continual" implies something that will go on forever. In other words, he knows she will not give up. It is a war of attrition. And so the judge will help the widow, not because he is just but because of her rope-a-dope tactics—because she will keep coming and because she will not get off his back until he gives her what she wants.

As in the earlier parable, a deceptively simple story from Jesus hides a complex theological theme that can be easily misinterpreted if one does not carefully think it through. Is this parable suggesting that God is like the capricious judge, rendering outcomes in prayer based on our determination to wear him out? Of course not. It is

---

11. The Greek word *hypōpiazō* occurs only twice in the New Testament: here and in 1 Corinthians 9:27, where the apostle Paul refers to the extreme discipline he exerts on his body so he might run in such a way as to win the prize—endurance.

12. Some early translations of the judge's comments end with him saying, "so that she may not finally come and slap me in the face."

13. Bailey, *Through Peasant Eyes*, 136.

important to understand that Jesus's parables on prayer emphasize more of *who God is* than the techniques of those who pray. Persistence is appropriate and even encouraged so that the one praying does not lose heart. But the point isn't that God is the sleeping neighbor or the impertinent judge. The point isn't that, if we bug God long enough, he will get fed up and do what we ask. That is pagan prayer, and misses the point of the parables.

Instead, if even a lowly widow's needs can be met by someone as heartless as the unjust judge, imagine *how much more* the needs of God's children will be supplied by a loving Father who has our best interests at heart! If even a sleepy, selfish neighbor will inconvenience himself only to preserve his honor, imagine *how much more* a loving Father will do to respond to our requests! The key is Jesus's revolutionary teaching about the *Abba* factor.

Jesus's first parable on prayer immediately follows the Lukan version of the Lord's Prayer, found in Luke 11:1–4. Similarly, following the parable of the friend at midnight, Jesus unfolds his explanation of prayer by describing the relationship between children who ask for help and loving parents who desire to take care of their children's needs. "Is there anyone among you who, if your child asks for a fish, will give a snake instead of a fish?" The unspoken answer is no. "Or if the child asks for an egg, will give a scorpion?" The obvious answer now is, *Of course not!* Jesus continues, "If you then, who are evil, know how to give good gifts to your children, *how much more* will the heavenly Father give the Holy Spirit to those who ask him!" (Luke 11:11–13, NRSV, emphasis added).

God is not like the cranky friend who is too tired to help. God is not like the heartless judge who is too uncaring to listen. We don't have to harangue God, impress God, or stroke God's ego to get him to listen to our prayers. Furthermore, if cranky friends and heartless judges eventually do what they are asked, how much more will the One who infinitely and eternally loves us listen to our hearts' cries? Thus, with twinkling eyes and a heartening smile, Jesus says: "So

I say to you: Ask and it will be given to you; seek and you will find; knock and the door will be opened to you" (11:9).

Could it be that we've made prayer more complicated than Jesus did? Does Jesus offer us a different way to pray?

Jesus's Teaching about Prayer

I see three fundamental aspects of Jesus's teaching on prayer.

1. Not Much Is Needed

Jesus's instruction in Matthew 6 is not a mandate to keep our prayers short. The Gospels highlight numerous times when Jesus spends entire nights praying. His concern is not the length of a person's prayers. Likewise, Jesus is not condemning formal prayers. As a Jewish boy, Jesus himself learned to pray the Psalms as a regular devotional habit and later gave us the Lord's Prayer as a guide. Formal prayers prayed with a sincere heart are not the problem.

What Jesus is trying to correct is the mistaken assumption that prayer is a way of twisting God's arm to do our bidding. "More is better" may be a pagan principle of prayer, but it is not a Christian one. To paraphrase: "The pagans babble on and on, thinking that many words equals good prayer. But I'm trying to tell you, *much* is only *more*. More isn't always bad, but even the smallest and seemingly insignificant prayers matter to God."

Some might push back by saying, *Wait, doesn't that only discourage people from praying?* Only if we don't understand the paradox that, when we are relieved of the burden of *much* in prayer, we experience the freedom of *more* in prayer.

Those who pray long, drawn-out prayers because they believe they have to for God to listen misunderstand the heart of God. However, few things encourage prayer like being released from the burden of many words to make it count. If prayer becomes yet another to-do item to check off a list, like mowing the lawn or taking out the garbage, then it's difficult to pray with gladness and devotion. When we begin to comprehend that not much is needed for us to have much of the Father, we breathe a sigh of relief and learn to rest and trust that we are in good hands.

2. God Already Knows

The reason not much is needed is that "your Father knows what you need before you ask him" (Matthew 6:8). Oswald Chambers calls this the root of all prayer.[14] Which raises the question: If God already knows our needs and what we are going to pray for, then why should we pray at all? Why ask?

I have discovered that in relationships with people who already know me—some who know me better than I know myself—I feel most comfortable to open up. Whenever prayer ends up sounding like an intelligence briefing on cable news, it is a sure sign we believe God is not quite up to speed. Does God need debriefings? Does God need to be informed of the minute details of every problem we are confronted with? David didn't think so: "Before a word is on my tongue you, LORD, know it completely" (Psalm 139:4).

Authentic prayer acknowledges that God knows what we need before we ask him, which knowledge frees us to be as direct and forthright as a four-year-old asking her mother for help. Complete assurance—absolute confidence. It also maintains the clear perspective that prayer is about more than getting things from God. It is being in communion with God. Or, as Chambers beautifully puts it, "I tell him what I know he knows in order that I may get to know it as he does."[15]

3. We Have an Eager Father

Jesus's teaching on prayer is permeated with the surprising revelation that we have a heavenly Father who is ready and willing to hear

---

14. Oswald Chambers, *Studies in the Sermon on the Mount: God's Character and the Believer's Conduct* (Grand Rapids: Discovery House Publishers, 1995), 51.

15. Chambers, *Studies in the Sermon on the Mount*, 51.

Jesus prays unlike anyone the disciples have ever known—almost as if he knows something they don't know or someone they don't recognize.

and answer our prayers. God isn't like the pagan gods. Our heavenly Father is not a reluctant listener. We don't have to keep running up to his chair, tugging on his pant leg, pulling the newspaper down from his face to get his attention. God never says: "What now? You know I just got home from work. I'm exhausted. I need some peace and quiet. Let me have some 'me' time, and we can talk later." No, this Father is always waiting with open arms, ready to listen, to know, and to act.

When we know that not much is required of us in order to have much of the Father, that is grace. When we believe that God knows our needs before we even speak them, that is intimacy. And when we comprehend that God is eager to hear from us, that is love.

Familiarity with and understanding of these three fundamentals is when we are liberated to *really* pray—not to talk about prayer, not to philosophize about prayer, but released to pray simply and joyfully. It takes all the pretense out of prayer. There is no need to pretend or bargain. We can be open, honest, and transparent with the God who already knows.

Jesus invites us to pray, "Our *Father*, who is in heaven." I'm afraid our familiarity with the Lord's Prayer has diminished the original force and wonder of those who first heard Jesus's teaching. The disciples observe Jesus's personal prayer life and notice how different it seems compared to their traditional understanding of the purpose and meaning of prayer. Remember, these disciples are young men who have already been trained to pray. They have been schooled in prayer. They pray the psalms regularly. As good Jewish boys, they pray faithfully four times a day at 9:00, 12:00, 3:00, and 6:00. They aren't asking Jesus to teach them to pray from scratch. They already understand the *function* of prayer. What they are asking Jesus to do is teach them to pray as he prays.

Jesus prays unlike anyone they have ever known—almost as if he knows something they don't know or someone they don't recognize.

I am convinced that is why Jesus doesn't focus on the nuts and bolts, formulas, and equations of prayer. His disciples already have those in spades. What they don't have is a firm grasp on whom they were praying to. So Jesus tells them stories about the Father's heart: the tender, fierce love of their heavenly Father who will never let them go and who is infinitely more patient and faithful than they could ever imagine or hope. Jesus knows that if he can pull back the curtain and let them see the heart of the Father for his children—a Father who doesn't make us beg, plead, or bargain—then prayer will come as naturally as breathing.

As parents, our children can come to us with the craziest requests. Sometimes we're amazed, even grieved, by the selfishness of what they ask for. But I think we would be sadder if they never came to us for help at all. I'm glad they come, mixed motives and all. I believe that's the way God is too. He listens with compassion and interest, just as we do in our best moments when our children come to us. Our heavenly Father is more moved by our neediness than by our eloquence; more moved by our simple trust than our perfect performance. Our words may be awkward, our attempts may be feeble, our motives may be misaligned, and our intentions may be confused—yet, because the power of prayer is not in the one who prays but in the One who hears, our prayers matter.

Our image of our Father will determine the way we pray. That is prayer according to Jesus.

PRACTICAL WAYS TO GROW IN PRAYER

We learn better when we learn by doing. We learn to pray best by praying. Books are helpful, and methods are useful. But the mystery and joy of prayer are discovered when we actually *do*. I know this should be obvious, but it is true: The more I pray, the more I rest; the more I rest, the less I try to control; the less I try to control, the more I feel in rhythm with grace. The focus of this chapter is practical ways to grow in prayer as a praying pastor.

My daily reflection and prayer routine usually begin around 5:30 a.m. (I'm a morning person). When I'm home, I start in my office chair with a cup of coffee, my study Bible, journal, and the devotional books I am currently using. I start with a prayer for enlightenment, asking the Holy Spirit to speak. Then I proceed with reading the scriptural lections for the day. Beyond that, the first hour of my day will vary between reading, writing, and praying. Listening to God comes easiest for me in that routine. My day is always better when it starts with God's words instead of the news cycle or social media. Exercise follows, then a light breakfast. But praying is only beginning. Now my mind and heart are better attuned to follow whatever guidance the Lord may choose to give me for the work that follows.

That's how I do it. My disclaimer is to remind you that, when it comes to spiritual practices, everyone is different. There is no right or wrong way to have personal daily time with God. You can use whatever is helpful as a model. The key is to find what works best for you. Only keep in mind that what feels like a rigorous discipline to start can become a holy habit one learns to depend on. Most importantly, I want you to know that God wants to meet with you and will give you the grace to do it. It is a discipline, but it is not legalistic. It requires effort (like all good things), but we do not *earn* God's love and favor by doing it—we *respond* to God's love and favor that are already ours.

#1 Find a Regular Place to Pray

I do not know of any pastor who envisions prayer as something to be checked off a task list, like "call Sister Wilson" or "finish prepping the worship bulletin." Leading real, flesh-and-blood congregations requires regular prayer, ongoing and often. Indeed, for every Christian, lay or clergy, prayer can become a way of being, of abiding in Christ and learning to live in an everyday and continual God-consciousness—an awareness of the presence of God in every moment. The phrase "practicing the presence of God" was made famous by Brother Lawrence, a simple Carmelite layman of the seventeenth century whose daily chores radiated prayer, whether he was peeling potatoes in the kitchen or repairing sandals. No doubt, this is akin to Paul's commendation to "pray continually" (1 Thessalonians 5:17), recognizing prayer as a way of life—or, as Wesley gracefully expressed, "the breath of our spiritual life."[1]

---

1. John Wesley, *Explanatory Notes upon the New Testament* (New York: G. Lane and C. B. Tippett, 1845), 5:16.

Obviously, one can learn to pray in any circumstance, no matter how challenging.[2] However, this does not invalidate the importance of having a designated time and place to pray. There is something about sacred space and intentional time for prayer that helps our concentration and perception. The old-timers used to call it "going into our prayer closet." They weren't recommending going into the place where we hang coats and store shoes. The prayer closet was a metaphor for a regular, quiet place set aside to be alone with God.

The concept is first introduced by Jesus, when he warns his disciples not to pray like hypocrites, who choose to pray in public places as though performing for a crowd. Jesus isn't saying that street-corner praying is bad—only that we must check our motives. Just as our giving should not be done to impress others, so our praying is to be done so that we keep our eyes on God instead of on people. Jesus instructs his followers to go into a closet and pray to the heavenly Father. Since the houses of Jesus's day were commonly one-room dwellings without closets, it seems obvious that Jesus is using a figure of speech to emphasize an important rule of Christian prayer: God knows what is done in secret and what is truly from the heart. Philip Yancey's assessment of Jesus's concept is enlightening: "[Jesus is] suggesting that we construct an imaginary room, a sanctuary of the soul, that fosters complete honesty before God. Though I need not find a literal closet, somehow I must ensure that my prayers are heartfelt and not a performance. That happens most conveniently in a closed room, but it may happen also in a church full of other people, or sitting with an elderly parent in a nursing home, or lying next to a spouse in bed."[3] A prayer closet need not be a physical construct or have absolute privacy, but it is about sacred space.

---

2. Martin Luther famously said, "There is no Christian who does not have time to pray without ceasing."

3. Yancey, *Prayer*, 33.

I have always been intrigued by the Exodus account of the first tabernacle: "Now Moses used to take a tent and pitch it outside the camp some distance away, calling it the "tent of meeting." Anyone inquiring of the LORD would go to the tent of meeting outside the camp" (33:7). For the sake of context, in a stunning turn of events, God reaches the point where the hardheartedness of the people makes it impossible for his presence to dwell in their midst. The LORD's holiness and Israel's sin cannot coexist. Thus Moses in effect decides: *If God isn't coming to where we are, then we're going to go where God is.* So he built a tabernacle outside the camp where he and whoever else wanted to could come and meet with God. In that tent of meeting (a beautiful description of a prayer closet), miraculous things begin to happen. When Moses enters the tent, God's presence descends in the form of a cloud and tangibly envelops the tent. There Moses learns to speak to God face to face, and gains a reputation with the people as the friend of God. Even when Moses returns to the camp, his young protégé, Joshua, lingers in the tent a little longer because (I assume) he doesn't want to leave the awesome Presence. Not coincidentally, this is also the place where Moses learns to intercede on behalf of the people (Exodus 33:12ff). It is a designated place to pray, to seek, and come to know the heart of God, a place that stands apart from the tumult of life in the main camp.[4]

Jesus's designated prayer closets are gardens and mountains. With his busy schedule, C. S. Lewis prayed traveling on trains, sitting on park benches, and walking city streets. One of my preferred prayer

---

4. Bonaventure wrote *The Character of a Christian Leader* in the thirteenth century, presumably to instruct heads of Christian communities. In that sense, it has become a classic text for the vocational spirituality of a pastor. In regard to the busy life of a spiritual leader, he alludes to Moses refreshing himself in the tent of meeting: "Moses, although taken up by duties to the people, often turned back to the Lord in the tent of the covenant. There he spoke personally with the Lord, finding refreshment for his spirit." St. Bonaventure, trans. Philip O'Mara, *The Character of a Christian Leader* (Ann Arbor, MI: Servant Books, 1978), 68.

closets is the golf course behind our house. I spend many early-morning hours prayer-walking the back nine before golfers tee off. Being outside in nature focuses my concentration and renews my mind and body. The demanding travel schedule in my current assignment does not make finding a regular place to pray easy, but when on the road, I am discovering the benefits of making the effort to look for prayer closets in hotel lobbies and deck chairs on hotel patios.

A minor digression but an important aspect of where we pray are the postures we take in prayer. Does it matter if one sits, kneels, bows, walks, clasps hands, or lies prostrate? Does it matter whether one's eyes are open or closed, head down or looking up? My answer may surprise you: yes, it does matter. It matters not because one is preferable to the other but because what we do with our bodies matters. We are more than spirits or souls—we are embodied persons, and as human beings, we express ourselves through our bodies. This is true not only of our daily interactions with others but also of the spiritual dimensions when we express ourselves to God. A curious interviewer once asked Rowan Williams if there is a specific way Christians should pray. His answer was sharply matter-of-fact for a person of his gravitas:

> We express ourselves in our bodies, don't we? I talk to you, and I wave my hands around a bit. My face changes, my body shifts. So, when I pray, I think it's worth asking, "What do I want to express?" Sometimes what I want to express is adoration, of letting go. You kneel, you bow to the ground, whatever, you lie flat on your face as some people do. Sometimes what you want to express is just listening, just attentiveness, you sit. You calm yourself, you center yourself, and you almost feel your ears growing, you know? And you breathe in and let God be there.[5]

---

5. Williams, interview for *Songs of Praise*, https://www.youtube.com /watch?v=S1RvKQU78zQ.

Williams indicates that what we want to express to God—including our capacity for listening in any given moment—will determine the physical position that is most appropriate for our prayer.

One of my favorite books of the prolific C. S. Lewis is a lesser-known work, *Letters to Malcolm: Chiefly on Prayer.* The last book written by Lewis, published posthumously, *Letters* is a series of correspondence with someone we assume is a fictional friend who has questions about the intricacies, joys, and struggles of prayer. In typical Lewis style, he writes with pungent wit, poignant honesty, and true-to-life experience with an unpretentious elegance that is relatable to the simplest of minds. When Malcolm asks about the appropriate posture for prayer, Lewis does not dodge the question: "When one prays in strange places and at strange times one can't kneel, to be sure. I won't say this doesn't matter. The body ought to pray as well as the soul. Body and soul are both the better for it. Bless the body. . . . The relevant point is that kneeling does matter, but other things matter even more. A concentrated mind and a sitting body make for better prayer than a kneeling body and a mind half asleep."[6] When Malcolm presses further on whether the time of day is important, Lewis makes fun of his own penchant for nodding off, while also reinforcing the power of deliberate concentration and eliminating distractions: "I entirely agree with you that no one in his senses, if he has any power of ordering his own day, would reserve his chief prayers for bed-time—obviously the worst possible hour for any action which needs concentration. . . . My own plan, when hard pressed, is to seize any time, and place, however unsuitable, in preference to the last waking moment."[7] The time, the place, and the postures of prayer all play a part in making the experience of prayer edifying. They will vary for every person. However, when we

---

6. Lewis, *Letters to Malcolm*, 17.
7. Lewis, *Letters to Malcolm*, 16.

give our best effort and time, we discover that the Lord is faithful to meet us there.

#2 Befriend Silence

Since the purpose of prayer is to know God and therein know ourselves, we come to realize that prayer is more than filling up the air with our words and telling God what we need or want. It is learning to rest in God's presence. We are usually silent in the presence of another if we are intimidated, awestruck, or comfortable enough not to feel the need to justify or defend ourselves. One is based on fear; one is based on spellbound amazement, and one is based on true friendship. I can measure the depths of my friendship with a person based on my willingness and ease with just being quiet when I'm with them. My wife and I often enjoy sitting in the same room or by our backyard firepit without the necessity of conversation. Sometimes we read, other times we pray, and occasionally we bird-watch. What we are doing isn't relevant. The point is, with or without words, we like being together. We prefer to do those things with each other rather than alone.

A pastor friend of mine once heard a Catholic sister say, "If you're looking for God, God is in the pause." That strikes me as important in a busy world: God meets us in the pause. "For God alone my soul waits in silence; from him comes my salvation" (Psalm 62:1, NRSV). Friends of God often meet him in the waiting room of silence.

The story of Elijah is instructive. After a long and arduous journey, literally running for his life, Elijah finds himself outside a cave on the ledge of a mountain. He desperately needs to hear from God. He is surprised to discover that God's voice is not heard in the wind, fire, or earthquake but in the gentle whisper of absolute silence (the Hebrew says, "there was a sound of fine silence"). In the pause, God is finally able to get Elijah's full attention and help him find his balance again.

Psalm 23 is undoubtedly one of David's most well-known psalms: "He makes me lie down in green pastures, he leads me beside quiet waters, he refreshes my soul" (vv. 2–3). David has learned that a life without lack is an attitude of mind formed in quiet moments with God. However, a more obscure psalm of David (just three verses long) is becoming my go-to text for the restorative power of being in the presence of God. Psalm 131 reads:

My heart is not proud, LORD,

my eyes are not haughty;

I do not concern myself with great matters

or things too wonderful for me.

But I have calmed and quieted myself,

I am like a weaned child with its mother;

like a weaned child I am content.

Israel, put your hope in the LORD

both now and forevermore.

So many of the psalms are written from the point of view of soldiers at the front lines. They contain urgent cries and highly emotional prayers. At times they seem more like screams than songs. Psalm 131 is different. David isn't shouting; he is resting. Things feel quiet, like the quiet in a room where a young mother is rocking her baby to sleep. It is a deep-breathing, non-anxious peace. David rests, content in God's presence, like a weaned child who is no longer restless and rooting to nurse at his mother's breast but instead is lying peacefully, satisfied simply to be near his mother, enjoying the closeness, at ease in her embrace.[8]

---

8. Because Psalm 131 is considered to be a song of ascent (on the way to worship, ascending Mount Zion to the temple), another metaphor some biblical scholars have employed here is that of a young child who has been carried by her mother on a long journey and is now being transferred into the strong arms of her father for the remainder of the trip. The Hebrew word used twice in verse 2 and translated as "with" most frequently means "upon." It is a beautiful image of trust and rest.

For men and women who stake our vocational claim as those who speak words (lots and lots of words), it can be difficult for pastors to see the usefulness of silence. When one spends so much time with a microphone in one's hand, it can be a challenge to hear anything but the sound of one's own voice. The practice of so little silence, combined with an inordinate desire for greatness and accomplishment, creates great restlessness and discontent for many church leaders. But here is David, at the pinnacle of his political prowess, if only for a moment humbly setting the self-comfort and self-talk aside. Borrowing phrases from the fertile imagination of Eugene Peterson, David is not trying to rule the roost, be king of the mountain, meddle where he has no business, or fantasize grandiose plans that he knows are in God's care. Instead, he cultivates a quiet heart as he waits in hope.[9] He sings a song of quiet trust.

I confess that I often approach God for what God can give me. And indeed, we are invited to ask when we are in need. But this psalm invites us to be silent before the LORD and to be comforted solely by his closeness and by the rest that comes from knowing we are loved. It is a time for being, not doing.

There is a story about a prisoner who fell asleep every time he came to worship services in the prison. The prison pastor once said to him, "Maybe it's not a good habit to sleep in church."

The prisoner gave him a wonderful answer: "You know, I am sick in the head, I can't get to sleep anywhere, and the only time my thoughts leave me alone is when I'm in church."

The only time he was completely at rest in his mind and body was in church, where he was secure in God's presence. He was not wrong. I believe he was experiencing the embodied reality of Psalm 131.

---

9. I am indebted to Eugene Peterson's imaginative paraphrase of Psalm 131 in *The Message*.

Similarly, one day a young man confessed to Pope Francis, "I sometimes fall asleep when I am at adoration."[10]

Francis replied, "It doesn't matter. God keeps looking at you."[11]

God's laser-focused attentiveness is nothing new: "You watched me as I was being formed in utter seclusion, as I was woven together in the dark of the womb" (Psalm 139:15, NLT). God has been watching us for a long time. Being under the watchful eye of God is peaceful rest—or trust. We experience this peace with God not by any merit or accomplishment of our own. We are restful because we know we are his children. Jesus experienced that same restfulness and reassured us that, like himself, we are the Father's beloved—generously and profoundly loved.

Brennan Manning tells the story of Edward Farrell, a priest from Detroit, who went to Ireland to visit relatives. On an early-morning walk with his eighty-year-old uncle along the shores of Lake Killarney, Farrell noticed that, although they weren't talking, his Uncle couldn't stop smiling.

"Uncle Seamus," Farrell said, "You look very happy. How come?"

To which the old Scotsman replied, gleefully, "The Father of Jesus is very fond of me."

When that truth becomes real for us, there is no need to be proud or pretentious, haughty or self-important. Only when we believe that God is our Father, who loves us as he loves Jesus, and that he extravagantly pours the same love upon us that he has for his Son from all eternity can we put an end to the false images of a critical, harsh, and

---

10. Adoration is the Roman Catholic practice of spending an hour focused on the worship of Jesus before receiving Eucharist—also called the Holy Hour [sanctus hora].

11. Pope Francis, Our Father: Reflections on the Lord's Prayer (New York: Penguin Random House, 2018), 41.

overly demanding God who would crush our spirits and discourage our prayers.

Pope Francis also admitted that he sometimes falls asleep in prayer. However, rather than finding this off-putting, the Father likes it when one of his children can fall asleep in his presence. It is a sign of a calm and quiet soul and, Francis believes, is one of the many ways to hallow God's name: to feel like a child in his hands.[12] I remember staring at my own babies while they slept in their cribs. It was the only time they were still enough for me to really study them. I was overwhelmed with a fierce love that determined not to let anything or anyone harm them. I was their father—they were my beloved.

Like Francis, I sometimes fall asleep when I pray. I used to feel guilty about my lack of focus; although it was unintentional, it felt like I was "giving in," and that God might be rolling his eyes at my surface-level commitment ("David, dost thou sleep? Couldst not thou watch one hour?"). Now I wonder if the Father looks at me and says, *Shhh. It's okay. You're with me now—I've got you.* This rings truer to me. When I can be quiet with such a Father, I feel like a child in his arms and can breathe in the fresh air of grace.

#3 Normalize Your Prayer Routine

The average contemporary Western person is addicted to activity. The right not to be bored has become an undisputed entitlement. With cell phones in hand and the miracle of unlimited data, distractions abound to assuage our attention disorder. Consequently, a spiritual virus has emerged known as "hurry sickness," and the outbreak has infected many pastors. From time to time, pastors point to their frenetic activity as a badge of honor or confirmation of their importance. "I'm so busy I can't even take a day off. I haven't had

---

12. Pope Francis, *Our Father*, 41–42.

a vacation in years." Being a hard worker is a good thing; being a workaholic is a disease.

There are warning signs of hurry sickness that pertain to the discipline of a daily devotional routine: incessantly checking the time; fighting the temptation (and often giving in) to check your phone; hastily scanning a scripture and, seconds later, having no idea what you just read; wishing you could be done so you can move on to the "more important" stuff of ministry. It is a truism to say one can be externally quiet and internally noisy. One can be utterly alone and completely preoccupied. These are a few of the symptoms of hurry sickness.

The pitfalls of hurry sickness abound, but none is more fatal than that hurry kills love for God and love for others. It is an undeniable fact that it's hard to love when we're in a hurry. "Love and hurry are fundamentally incompatible," John Ortberg wrote. "Love always takes time, and time is the one thing hurried people don't have."[13] Hurried people are impatient and easily angered. They are edgy, and they find it hard to make time to listen and be present with others; they see people but not persons. Relationships become to-do lists at best and distractions at worst.

For that reason, hurry is a poison for pastoral care. It doesn't mean a pastor cannot be busy—it means a pastor cannot be hurried. I honestly do not personally know a pastor who doesn't want that kind of balance. The problem isn't desire—it's a lack of margin. When the margins are so thin that fifteen extra minutes with a hurting person throws our whole day into a tailspin, something is out of balance. Usually, the first thing to go is regular time alone with God. Normalizing a routine is one of the cures for hurry sickness.

A brief glimpse into the daily life of Jesus attests to the fact that he usually had a lot to do. But I am also struck by the fact that he never seems disconnected from his Father or uninterested in people.

---

13. John Ortberg, *The Life You've Always Wanted: Spiritual Disciplines for Ordinary People* (Grand Rapids: Zondervan, 2002), 81.

We learn to pray best

by praying.

Maybe that's why we have so many instances of Jesus withdrawing (usually early in the morning or late at night) for time alone with God. As a result, Jesus can be busy without being hurried—active while remaining centered. He is mindful of his schedule without being a slave to it. I can't help but think that Jesus's intentional practice of time to quiet his heart keeps his activity rightly ordered. When we complain that we do not have enough time, we can follow Jesus's example to "learn to do expeditiously what has to be done in order to get on to what *must* be done."[14]

By the time we reached the one-year mark of the coronavirus pandemic, most organizations, including churches, had moved from crisis mode into adaptive mode. Yet many pastors still struggled to adjust, living in a constant state of exhaustion and trying to keep "normal" things happening in an abnormal time without an end in sight. A recent Eblin Group blog distinguishes between fatigue and depletion. Fatigue applies to one's mind and body while depletion deals more with one's emotional and spiritual state. A person can be both fatigued *and* depleted, but one leads to the other, and each one requires a different antidote. Fatigue can be treated with rest and relaxation, but depletion requires the restoration of what has been drained away.[15] Said in another way, in this unusual time, pastors need more than a vacation; they need to be replenished.

God doesn't intend for any of us to live with our hair on fire. More activity can be energizing, adrenaline-infusing, and even productive when it revolves around the church we love, the friends we know, and the service we are trained to do. But it is possible to fall into a monotonous rut of religious activity without any real replenishment of our spirit. Only those closest to us can usually see the effect, but we slowly begin to sense the Spirit of God being suppressed

---

14. Neuhaus, *Freedom for Ministry*, 206, emphasis added.

15. Scott Eblin, "New Year, Same Boat?" *Eblin Group Blog*, January 12, 2021, https://eblingroup.com/blog/new-year-same-boat/.

in us. We begin to feel the numbing ache of the soul that indicates something is missing. If we feel out of control, even to the point of breakdown, there is a way to slow down and be renewed. Burnout is *not* inevitable for pastors. Hurry sickness need not be terminal. When we sigh over more meetings, more expectations, and more deadlines, we have the power to rearrange and reprioritize our routines. Unhurried time spent with our Father is where and when we learn to live by the rhythms of grace.

#4 Recognize That Prayer Forms Us

We must embrace the truth that prayer is not something we master. Hopefully, all of us are continually maturing in our understanding of prayer, but no one graduates from the school of prayer. Yet the very act of prayer is formational.

Of course, not every quiet time with God will consist of rushing wind and blazing fire falling from heaven. If our expectation every time we pray is for an overwhelming, numinous-awe, emotional experience, we will be disappointed. It is safe to assume Peter does not see a sheet descend from heaven every time he observes the hours of prayer. He sees the vision in God's time because it is his custom to pray at noon (Acts 10). When Isaiah sees the Lord enthroned and holy, with thresholds shaking and smoke filling the house, it is because he goes to the temple for worship and prayer, as he has so many times before (Isaiah 6). Theophanies most often happen in the ordinary aspects of life.

When Oswald Chambers wrote that "drudgery is the test of genuine character," he simply meant that being willing to do what is right even when we don't feel like it is the sign of a sanctified disposition.[16] No one is born with character; it must be developed. Just as we are not born with preconceived habits, so God-glorifying habits are

---

16. Oswald Chambers, *My Utmost for His Highest*, June 15, https://utmost .org/get-moving-2/.

developed via intentional practices. There are many times in prayer when there are no flashes of inspiration or life-transforming visions, but that doesn't mean nothing is happening to us. The very discipline of praying when we don't feel like it forms us into a certain kind of person. Like all spiritual practices, acts of love that are reinforced by a decision of the will have a long-term effect that is rarely realized in the moment.

Dorothy Day entrenched her life in serving the poor, the sick, the marginalized, and the oppressed. She often worked long days, from seven in the morning until late at night. After such exhausting days she was tempted to forego her evening prayers. On one particular day that had been full of activity, she wrote in her journal, "If you have to force yourself to pray, those prayers are of far more account with God than any prayers that bring comfort with them. That act of will is *very* important."[17] When we pray, and we are not seeking comfort or consolation, it is an act of love toward God and others. Perhaps these acts of the will delineate between a pastor who prays and a praying pastor. Then again, I suspect this is true of all pastoral ministry: "When we least feel like praying, we most need to pray; when study seems unfruitful, we need the more intensely to study; and when thinking is dead-ended, think again."[18]

The idea that the discipline of prayer takes away from the intimacy of prayer is misleading. Right practices lead to healthy habits. Practice is continually doing that which no one sees or knows except ourselves and God. Habit is the ongoing result of regular practice. Only in doing something regularly can it become second nature. Prayer can become a habit without becoming ritualistic. We can turn our very lives into prayer.

17. Dorothy Day, *The Reckless Way of Love: Notes on Following Jesus* (Walden, NY: Plough Publishing House, 2017), 48.

18. Neuhaus, *Freedom for Ministry*, 225.

When you're really in love with someone, you want to share your whole life with them. When something good happens to us, what's the first thing we want to do? We want to call the most important person in our lives and tell them about it. The opposite is also true: when something *isn't* going well, we want to call the most important person in our lives for encouragement. Just hearing their voice is a comfort. In good times and bad, they are constantly on our minds. I envision our relationship with God in the same way. We can simply enjoy his presence. We don't have to be formal to do that. We don't have to be in church to do that. We can be aware of his presence and rest in each moment like two persons who love each other. Oswald Chambers perceptively writes, "Prayer does not equip us for the greater work—prayer *is* the greater work."[19]

#5 Pray the Words of the People of God

Pietistic tradition has exalted extemporaneous prayer over written prayer. The former seems more spiritual, more from the heart; the latter seems more formal, more cold. Sincerity, so the thinking goes, trumps content. Yet it bears repeating that the most famous formal prayer in the history of formal prayers is the one Jesus taught us to pray. It is hard to argue against the value of the Lord's Prayer as a model and guide. This does not negate the importance of free, spontaneous prayer. It is better to say that formal prayer *informs* informal prayer. For example, when we begin our prayers with Scripture, we are more likely to pray theocentric (God-centered) prayers than egocentric ones. We should not do less than actually learning to pray the Scriptures (including the Psalms), but we should also do more—because, by definition, any reference to daily prayer must be biblical.

---

19. Chambers, *My Utmost*, October 17, https://utmost.org/the-key-of-the -greater-work/.

A systematic reading of the Bible and prayerful meditation go hand in hand. Part of my daily prayer time includes reading the historic Daily Office every morning as a way to immerse myself in God's Word that is not subject to my momentary whims or preferences. Instead, the Daily Office connects me with millions of fellow believers, past and present, in a comprehensive plan to address the whole of Scripture. This both precedes and accompanies how, what, and for whom I pray. When I am tempted toward subjective prayer, meditating on the Bible raises my viewpoint to more objective concerns.

Further, I find great help and encouragement in reading the prayers of fellow Christians. In his extremely rich yet practical book on prayer, Timothy Keller stresses that daily private prayer should be more interwoven with the corporate prayer of the church. John Wesley encouraged both formal and informal prayer. The guides to prayer he prepared for his preachers (ordained and lay) included collects from earlier church fathers and mothers (Wesley's Covenant Renewal Service is a prime example). Calvin, Luther, Knox, Cranmer, and others did the same, showing how important it was for the great teachers of the church that our prayer life not be completely privatized.[20]

In a time when biblical literacy is at an all-time low, it seems especially important for congregations to hear biblical sermons on prayer—and that they see, hear, and learn to pray thoughtful and celebrated historic prayers in public worship. If the only prayers our people hear are off-the-cuff prayers by worship leaders between songs or benedictory prayers to close a service, that is how they will begin to pray in private. It will not sustain their attempts at an ongoing and fruitful prayer life. That is why pastoral prayers are so important. Pastoral prayers can be both inspiring and instructive and,

---

20. Timothy Keller, *Prayer: Experiencing Awe and Intimacy with God* (New York: Dutton, 2014), 246.

as such, should be carefully and prayerfully thought through before the moment in which they are prayed.

I recall hearing Jeannie McCullough being called to the platform to pray during an evening worship service when I was a young ministerial student. From memory, she prayed personally and corporately through Psalm 139. When her prayer was finished I noticed that, although no explicit invitation had been issued, there were several people kneeling at the altar. I was moved to realize that expounding the psalm in a real-life moment of prayer had deeply touched the spirit of the people. They were given the words to pray about the things they wanted to pray for but had no way to articulate themselves. The psalm Jeannie prayed that night gave them a new kind of "grammar."[21]

What if the first words from the worship leader to begin a service were not, "How ya'll doin' today?" but, "Almighty God, unto whom all hearts are open, all desires known, and from whom no secrets are hidden: cleanse the thoughts of our hearts by the inspiration of your Holy Spirit, that we might perfectly love you and worthily magnify your holy Name. Through Jesus Christ our Lord." And what if the last words the congregation heard before departing the worship service were, "To him who is able to keep you from stumbling and to present you before his glorious presence without fault and with great joy—to the only God our Savior be glory, majesty, power and authority, through Jesus Christ our Lord, before all ages, now and forevermore! Amen" (Jude 1:24–25). Would these prayers cause leaders to stop praying their own spontaneous prayers? Would their vision for the power of prayer shrink? I doubt it very much. I have much greater confidence it would serve to open up their prayer imagination and lead them toward greater heights.

---

21. "Immersing ourselves in the Psalms and turning them into prayers teaches our hearts the grammar of prayer and gives us the most formative instruction in how to pray in accord with God's character and will." Keller, *Prayer*, 255.

Pastoral prayers can be both inspiring and instructive and, as such, should be carefully and prayerfully thought through before the moment in which they are prayed.

#6 Trust That God Welcomes Your Prayers

It has already been noted that Jesus's prayer life was markedly different from the ways other Jewish children were taught to pray in the synagogue. His style was more personal, less distant, and uncomfortably intimate. There had grown up in ancient Israel a deep reverence for the name of YHWH, their God (the four consonants used without the vowels is called the *Tetragrammaton*). So holy was this name considered to be that they dared not even speak it, much less *mis*use it. Through the various phases of Israel's history, especially during the post-exilic days of Ezra and Nehemiah, it became the custom to use other titles for God. Therefore, whenever they translated Scripture, they were careful to write the name Yahweh, but they never said it out loud. Even in the synagogues, when they came to the name Yahweh in Scripture, they would not say the name; instead, they said *Adonai*, which means "the Lord."[22]

Can you even imagine, then, the shock of hearing Jesus call God his *"Abba"*? The first recorded words of Jesus in Luke's Gospel are when he is twelve years old. It is Passover season in a crowded Jerusalem. His parents temporarily lose him. When they find him three days later sitting in the temple, they are justly worried and frustrated. Jesus's response to them is disconcerting: "Why were you searching for me? Didn't you know I had to be in my Father's house?" (Luke 2:49). At the tender age of twelve, he is referring to God as his *Abba*. Where has he learned that? Who in all of Israel has ever used such familiar terms as "father" or "papa" or "dad" for the holy name of God? And Jesus continues to do this for the rest of his life (Luke 11:2; 22:42; 23:46).

---

22. The Gospel writers give evidence of this. It is no problem for Luke, who is Greek, to write "the kingdom of God." But it is a deep problem for Matthew, who is Jewish, because ever since he was a little boy he was taught to revere that name. Therefore, Matthew does not write "the kingdom of God;" instead, he writes "the kingdom of heaven."

No one in the Old Testament directly addresses God as "Father," but Jesus is recorded as doing so 170 times. Even though there are many superlative prayers in the Hebrew Scriptures, they are not this intimate or immediate (David's psalms come the closest). "Some scholars," Philip Yancey notes, "suggest that Jesus virtually invented private prayer."[23] Whether that is the case, I cannot confirm. But this much I know: the way Jesus prayed was different. This was a new way to pray—this was the stuff of revolutions. Yancey continues, "The model prayer he gave deals with the stuff of daily life—God's will, food, debts, forgiveness, temptation—and his own prayers showed a spontaneous communion with the Father that had no precedent. His disciples, no novices at prayer themselves, marveled at the difference. 'Teach us to pray,' they asked."[24]

Yes, Jesus invites us to pray with persistence and boldness. But, *whom are we praying to?* is as important a question as, *what are we praying for?* The Father of Jesus is one who always welcomes us with open arms. "Who one believes God to be is most accurately revealed not in any credo but in the way one speaks to God when no one else is listening."[25] There is no need to bargain or beg or break down the door. After all, he is our Father too.

When we pray to *invoke* God, we are also *evoking*. To invoke means "to appeal to someone with authority," namely, God. To evoke means "to bring to mind." Consider the blessing before a meal. We don't pray before meals because we're afraid we'll get indigestion if we don't. We don't pray before meals for protection from our food (although college students in school cafeterias may disagree). No, we pray in those times as a way to pause the normal routines of our lives, to remember that God is with us and to acknowledge that our Father

23. Yancey, *Prayer*, 63.

24. Yancey, *Prayer*, 63.

25. Nancy Mairs, *Ordinary Time: Cycles in Marriage, Faith, and Renewal*, (Boston: Beacon Press, 1993), 54.

makes it all possible. That is evoking—calling to mind—what kind of God we pray to, reminding ourselves of the Trinitarian nature of God: God is our Father, and he is committed to our good. Jesus gives us access to the throne of the universe because he is our mediator, advocate, and priest. The Holy Spirit is God himself within us prompting and helping us to pray so we can know that, if we are praying, God is listening.[26]

I used to think prayer was mainly for noble concerns. I felt a gap between what I thought I should be praying for and what I was actually thinking about. It was easy for me to become distracted and think about all kinds of different things while I was praying. I felt like I should be praying for world evangelism, but I would find my mind drifting toward a difficult meeting I had the next day. I felt I should be praying for peace in the Middle East, but I couldn't quit thinking about my kids at school. I knew it was important to pray for the big stuff, but the smaller, more personal matters dominated my attention. I wondered if God might be getting impatient that I wasn't more selfless and magnanimous. I expected God might get fed up with subjecting himself to my petty appeals and demands, interrupt me, and say: *Timeout, David. Can we talk about something more important?* But, unsurprisingly, God is always patient with my small-mindedness, and graciously receives my requests.

I am learning that nothing kills prayer faster than when we pretend, in prayer, to be something we're not. "In prayer," C. S. Lewis wrote, "we must lay before him what is in us, not what *ought* to be in us."[27] God wants us to be honest and real with him; we are *Abba's* child.

Recasting Jesus's insights on prayer from Matthew 7 and Luke 11 can be helpful to me.

When one of my kids comes to me and says, "Dad, I'm hungry. Can I have a snack?" I don't say to them, "Well, maybe if you cared a

---

26. Keller, *Prayer*, 248.
27. Lewis, *Letters of Malcolm*, 22–23.

little more about starving children in the world, you would eat all of your dinner and stop asking for snacks."

Or, when one of my kids comes to me and says, "Dad, I'm really worried about such and such," I don't say, "What could you possibly be worried about? You're in ninth grade! Wait until you're a grown-up. Then you'll really have important stuff to worry about."

Of *course* I don't say those things. I *want* them to tell me what's on their mind, including their worries, disappointments, and joys. Maybe they do need to grow up some; maybe they do need to be thinking more about other people who are less fortunate than they are. But the bottom line is, I want them to tell me their concerns and share their burdens. If what they are asking for is something that will be good for them and it's within my power to give it to them, I will do everything I can to help them. Do you think our "how much more" Father would do less?

Corrie ten Boom is reported to have said, "Any concern too small to be turned into prayer is too small to be made into a burden." We can talk to God about what concerns us. Over time, as we grow up in God, our circles of concern also enlarge. Moreover, as we live in perpetual prayer relationship with God, we increasingly become more interested in the needs of others and the greater needs of the world. But as we learn to pray for those big-picture concerns, we can also tell God that we're frustrated with our coworker at the office; we can tell him that we're struggling to get along with someone at school; we can ask him to help us make our house payment. That's how intimate prayer can be. When we know our Father is waiting with open arms, we begin to count on the closeness.

Unanswered Prayer

One last thing to consider is our unanswered prayers. Is there even such a thing?

As far as I know, Jesus never mentioned unanswered prayer. Most of Scripture tilts the other way (Matthew 7:7; 18:19; 21:22; John

5:15–16, 15:7; Hebrews 4:16; James 5:15–16; 1 Peter 3:12; 1 John 5:14). I have heard it said that God answers every prayer in one of three ways: yes, no, or wait. I think there is wisdom in that. But there is a deeper truth here too. While we may not understand the unfathomable depths of prayer, we can hang on to something bigger than our questions: any answered prayer is because God is good, and any seemingly unanswered prayer is also because God is good.

Faith in our "how much more" Father believes that either our prayer will be answered or that something better will be given instead. God will either give us what we ask, or give us what we would have asked if we knew everything God knows.[28] Submission to God means that, even as we pray for certain things, we trust God's wisdom and goodness to do what is best for us. We can pray with confidence, knowing that our requests will be granted—or, if they are not, that their granting would not be good for us.

---

28. I first heard this statement in a sermon by Tim Keller. I would reference it here if I could remember when. I thank him for the idea.

INTERCESSION:
WHAT IT IS

"Intercession" is a common word in Christian vernacular, mostly connected to intercessory prayer. To intercede is to act on behalf of or to stand in the gap for someone.

I have always believed in the necessity of intercession and in the power that comes from it. But if I'm honest, I have to admit that some of my perceptions about intercession were off. Even as a pastor, I entertained reductionist ideas that everyone should pray but that the *real* intercessors—those who were called to the *ministry* of intercession—were either elderly or monastic; people who had the time and unique calling to pray for hours on end each day. Those of us who actually had to make a living and get things done counted on those other two groups to cover the rest of us with intercessory prayer. I was so wrong. The next two chapters are devoted to telling you why.

The venerable E. M. Bounds wrote nine books on the subject of prayer. I am captured by his statement, "Prayer in its highest form and grandest success assumes the attitude of a wrestler with God."[1]

---

1. E. M. Bounds, *Purpose in Prayer* (London: Marshall Bros., 1914), https://ccel.org/ccel/bounds/purpose/purpose.VI.html.

"Wrestler" is an interesting word choice. Those things that matter most in life are not gained without a struggle. They are hard-won and more cherished because they come at great personal cost and sacrifice. It is not by accident that God's people were given a name to remind them that they are the ones who strive with God.[2] Only after Jacob's terrifying wrestling match with a mysterious stranger in the night was he renamed and given a new identity (Genesis 32:28).

Comfort is never the path to a transformed life. We must be wrestled into finally understanding that God is the true source of the blessing we've been looking for. However, wrestling with God in prayer is the opposite of determinism ("It's going to happen any-way") or resignation ("I give up"). It is holding fast to the character of God in the face of every contradictory emotion or situation and saying, "I will not let you go unless . . ." (Genesis 32:26). The goal of prayer is not to try and overcome God's unwillingness to help us or to wear God down until he relents and intervenes. Rather, inter-cessory prayer is cooperating with God's highest will and greatest intentions for the world. That is why I agree so strongly with Wal-ter Wink's account of intercessory prayer: "History belongs to the intercessors—those who believe and pray the future into being."[3] Active and involved prayer can open our eyes to new possibilities that we could not imagine before.

Before we move to the application of intercessory prayer in the life of a praying pastor, I want us to consider the first recorded mono-theistic intercessor. His name is Abraham. He presents the first example of intercessory prayer in Scripture. This is how it all got started.

---

2. Israel literally means "God wrestler," "the one who strives with God," or "the one who struggles with God."

3. Walter Wink, *Engaging the Powers* (Minneapolis: Fortress Press, 1992), 301.

Abraham's Intercession

Genesis 18 is a remarkable story of the power of intercessory prayer. As is always the case, context is important. Abraham is sitting outside his tent near the oaks of Mamre, not far from Hebron, trying to stay cool in the heat of the day. Abraham is surprised to look up and see three travelers approach. They are strangers; he doesn't recognize them. Yet they come and stand near his campsite (the Middle Eastern equivalent of ringing a doorbell).

Abraham jumps to his feet (as much as a ninety-nine-year-old man can jump) and greets them with great hospitality, treating them like royalty. He bows low to the ground, putting himself in the place of a servant. He asks them to rest in the shade of the trees while he brings cool water to wash their dirty feet and food to refresh their bodies. The meal he brings is a feast for a king, the best he has to offer—prime rib, hand-selected from his herd.

But here is what's so interesting about the scene: up to this point, Abraham has no idea who these mystery guests are. We (the readers) know because verse 1 says, "The LORD appeared to Abraham." We have the advantage of knowing this is a physical manifestation of Yahweh God and that the other two men are angels in disguise on their way to get a firsthand look at Sodom. But Abraham doesn't know all this. He addresses the leader of the trio as "my lord" (lowercase "l"). It is a common courtesy, a way of showing respect, but he doesn't know it is actually *the* LORD (capital "L"). The point is, Abraham treats them like royalty before he realizes he is in the presence of *the* King.[4]

---

4. Perhaps this is the story the writer of Hebrews has in mind when writing on the importance of mutual love: "Do not neglect to show hospitality to strangers, for by doing that some have entertained angels without knowing it" (13:2, NRSV). One must be careful not to casually overlook anyone, no matter how seemingly insignificant.

When does Abraham recognize he is in the presence of the LORD?

Is it when the stranger asks, "Where is your wife Sarah?" (v. 9). It is one thing for a mystery guest to know the name of your wife—particularly since she has not come out of the tent to be introduced—but who except God would know that her name was changed from Sarai to Sarah?

Or is it when the mystery guest says, "I will surely return to you about this time next year, and Sarah your wife will have a son" (v. 10). The mystery guest also knows they are childless and Sarah barren. Perhaps Abraham's heart beats a little faster when he realizes these three are more than mere mortals, and one of them is the manifest presence of the LORD God Almighty.

After the meal, the three men who are no longer strangers resume their journey along the road to Sodom. Abraham walks with them for a time. Then, in a stunning revelation, the narrator reveals the thoughts of God's heart at that moment: "Shall I hide from Abraham what I am about to do?" (v. 17).

Sodom has become a place of terrible corruption, evil, and injustice, and God is going to do something about it. But apparently, no one except the emissaries with him knows the plan. God decides to share his planned judgment of Sodom with Abraham. Why would God want Abraham to know? Why would God even feel obligated to tell Abraham his intentions? I can think of only one reason: Abraham is God's friend.

The LORD answers his own question: "For I have chosen him, so that he will direct his children and his household after him to keep the way of the LORD by doing what is right and just, so that the LORD will bring about for Abraham what he has promised him" (v. 19). The intriguing phrase "keep the way of the LORD" is highlighted by two important Hebrew words: *tzedakah* and *mishpat*—"righteousness" and "justice." These are not impersonal principles of universal ethics or strict moral codes. They are covenantal, relational words.

They portray living all of our relationships in the way God intended, thereby making right what has gone wrong in God's world. God knows that Abraham will "keep the way of the LORD," and if Abraham is to be the father of "a great and powerful nation" (v. 18) through which all the nations of the world will be blessed, he needs to know God's mind.

So God tells his covenant friend what he intends to do in Sodom, and then the scriptural translation becomes debatable. The original language either says, "Abraham remained standing before the LORD," or it says, "the LORD remained standing before Abraham" (v. 22).[5] In some ways it doesn't matter because what happens next is beautiful.

When God first cut a covenant with Abraham, the LORD's presence came in the form of a smoking fire pot and a flaming torch, traversing between the pieces of the sacrificed animals. This action was the equivalent of God invoking a curse upon himself if he failed to fulfill his covenantal promises. Then God sealed it by walking through the divided carcasses in place of Abraham (see Genesis 15). Abraham was paralyzed with great fear and dread in a dreamlike state. Sometime later, the LORD appeared to him again and said, "I am God Almighty (*El Shaddai*); walk before me faithfully and be blameless" (17:1). This time Abraham responded by falling prostrate before the LORD.

In chapter 18, something different happens: "Abraham remained standing before the LORD," and Abraham even "approached" the

---

5. Walter Brueggemann references an early authoritative and authentic text note that shows Genesis 18:22 originally saying, before any translation, "Yahweh stood before Abraham." Brueggemann states, "It is as though Abraham presided over the meeting. But that bold image of Yahweh being accountable to Abraham for this theological idea was judged by the early scribes as irreverent and unacceptable. Therefore, the text was changed to read as we have it." Walter Brueggemann, *Genesis, Interpretation: A Bible Commentary for Teaching and Preaching* (Atlanta: John Knox Press, 1982), 168.

LORD (18:22, 23)! There is a marked progression in Abraham's understanding of his covenant relationship with God. In his previous encounters with the self-revealing disclosures of the LORD, Abraham has appropriately feared and revered God, but now there is something more that can only be identified as trust and intimacy. Here, Abraham speaks boldly to the LORD. He is not irreverent, but he is surprisingly candid: "Will you sweep away the righteous with the wicked?" (v. 23). *Will the fate of the wicked also be the fate of the righteous? Will you treat them the same?* "What if there are fifty righteous people in the city? Will you really sweep it away and not spare the place for the sake of the fifty righteous people in it?" (v. 24).

Some might view Abraham's questions as brazen impertinence: *Does Abraham know whom he's talking to? Does he think he is God's theological teacher? He's got a lot of nerve negotiating with God!* Some may hold this view, but apparently God does not. Not only does God not disapprove, but God also seems to welcome the interaction. Moreover, God has come to Abraham! God is there to talk with him, indeed, has invited conversation. Before, God appeared to Abraham in various theophanies that were mysterious and awe-inspiring. Now, God shows up in human form, sits down near Abraham's tent, shares a meal with him, and tells Abraham what he is thinking. It cannot be understated that God has allowed and even welcomed this progression of the relationship.

Abraham is not presumptuous. He knows he is still speaking to God and not a bowling buddy. He respects God's power, authority, and dominion even as he dares to believe God has invited him into a dialogue and wants to hear what he thinks. *Will you spare the city for fifty righteous people?* "The LORD said, 'If I find fifty righteous people in the city of Sodom, I will spare the whole place for their sake'" (v. 26).

The rest of the conversation is nothing short of astonishing.
Can I be so bold as to ask if you will save it for forty-five?
"I will not destroy it if I find forty-five there" (v. 28, NRSV).

Will you save it for forty?

"For the sake of forty, I will not do it" (v. 29).

Don't be angry, but will you save it for thirty?

"I will not do it if I find thirty there" (v. 30).

Suppose there are twenty?

"For the sake of twenty, I will not destroy it" (v. 31).

Forgive me, but could I ask one more question? Will you save it for ten?

"For the sake of ten, I will not destroy it" (v. 32).

Though this is a thumbnail sketch of the actual conversation, it serves to underscore the stunning nature of intercession when undergirded by intimate trust. From where does this friendship derive? It commenced in God's choosing of Abraham to be a blessing to the nations (Genesis 12), and comes to full expression in 18:19, where the same word is used for "chosen" as is found in Proverbs 3:6: *yâda'*, "to know."[6] Because God "knows" Abraham, he has chosen him and allowed him access to cosmic conversations. And because Abraham "knows" God, he can ask risky questions and intercede with the bold posture of a friend.

Abraham is not bargaining with God, nor is he cutting a deal. This isn't negotiation; this is intercession—prayer at the deepest level. Abraham isn't trying to modify God's sense of justice; he doesn't assume to be more righteous or compassionate than God. He is calling on God to *be* who God already *is*. Can you see the implications for prayer?

The hope of God in the blessing of Abraham is taking form. God has promised to make him a blessing to all the peoples of the

---

6. The Hebrew text of Genesis 18:19 literally reads, "For I have *known* him as my own so that he may teach and command his children . . ." Further, in typical Hebrew narrative irony, the term *yâda'* is used in 19:5, when the men of Sodom demand that the two visitors be brought out so that they might "know" them, and again in 19:8, when Lot offers his two daughters who have not yet "known" a man (virgins)—hence the dual meaning of *yâda'* to know another intimately.

world, and here we are given its shape in full bloom. This is a break-through of epic proportion—a shift in humanity never before seen—because God finally has a man who is concerned for more than his own well-being. At last, God has a human being showing compassion for more than family or clan. Here is one who cares even for the most wicked of his generation. Abraham is standing in the gap for Sodom.

He isn't asking God to spare ten righteous people. He is asking God to spare all of Sodom *for the sake of* ten righteous people.[7] I have no doubt this has been God's desire all along. After all, God is the one who called Abraham to be a blessing and to do righteousness and justice in the world. Abraham is reflecting the heart of God through intercessory prayer. This state of Abraham's heart didn't happen overnight. It has been twenty-four years in the making, with some fits and starts and an occasional mess (cf. Genesis 12:10–20; 16:1–15). But now Abraham is a friend of God, who "knows" God and can pray with a knowledge that is consistent with God's character.

The heart of all true intercession is having the heart of God for the world. It is standing in the gap for people we may not personally know and who are not like us.[8] Why? Because we care about that which troubles God. Perhaps that is why intercessory prayer is one of the deepest levels of intimacy we can have with God—because now it's not just about me; it's about God's will being done on earth as it is in heaven. It's about an intimacy that allows for our concerns to become God's and for God's concerns to become ours—a familiarity where the lines have become blurred in the knowing. In the words of Tim Stafford, "We do not pray to tell God what he does not

---

7. No matter how great the odds against them, never underestimate the redemptive power of a few righteous persons.

8. "Only eternity will reveal how many times judgment has been avoided by the intercession of the saints." H. Ray Dunning, *Abraham: The Tests of Faith* (Kansas City, MO: Beacon Hill Press of Kansas City, 2012), 96.

know, nor to remind him of things he has forgotten. He already cares for the things we pray about. He has simply been waiting for us to care about them with him. When we pray, we stand by God and look with him toward those people and problems."[9]

Imagine that. God invites us into his inner circle.

The Nature of Intercession

The example of Abraham helps define the nature of intercession: to pray on behalf of or to stand in the gap for someone. The apostle Paul picks up on this theme when he observes the praying life of Epaphras in the Colossian church: "Epaphras, who is one of you and a servant of Christ Jesus, sends greetings. *He is always wrestling in prayer for you*, that you may stand firm in all the will of God, mature and fully assured" (Colossians 4:12, emphasis added).

While there are many good explanations of intercession, I have developed my own definition: *Intercession is specifically praying for those God has providentially placed in our circle of relationships and sphere of influence.* Every word and phrase is intentional, with a particular focus on three: "specifically," "providentially," and "circle of relationships."

The nature of intercession is *specific*. When people say they pray daily for all the missionaries in Africa or hungry children in India, I am thankful for their concern and their prayers, but I don't consider that intercession. Biblical intercession is focused on particulars, not generalities. Details are the stuff of intercession. According to Dietrich Bonhoeffer, "It is clear that intercessory prayer is not general and vague but very concrete: a matter of definite persons and definite difficulties, and therefore, of definite petitions. The more

---

9. Tim Stafford, *Knowing the Face of God* (Grand Rapids: Zondervan, 1986), 134.

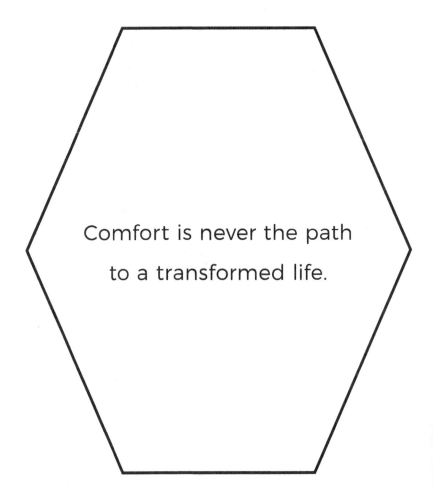

Comfort is never the path
to a transformed life.

definite my intercession becomes, the more promising it is."[10] By "definite," Bonhoeffer means "specific."

Intercession is interested in *specific* persons and *specific* difficulties and, therefore, *specific* requests. The more concrete our intercessory prayer becomes, the more promising it is. Generic prayers for "those in need" are not bad. This may be the way young Christians learn to pray. But the Holy Spirit is faithful to help us hone in with greater specificity as we grow in our understanding of intercessory prayer. The reason for this is very important: love sees faces. Love sees real people with real needs, including the good, the bad, and the ugly. Love requires us to bear on our hearts the burden of those for whom we pray. That is why it's easier to pray for a friend than a stranger. We know the details of their lives. We see their hopes and dreams, fears and pain. When we know the details, vagueness disappears. Intercession sees faces so we can pray in specifics.

The gift of intercession also requires *discernment*. Discernment is different than knowledge or wisdom. Knowledge has to do with information and facts. It includes one's intellectual capacity, smarts, and IQ. We gain knowledge through education, academics, and reading. Wisdom is the capability of knowing how to use one's knowledge in practical ways. Having several degrees on the wall doesn't ensure common sense (we all know really smart people who have zero wisdom). Discernment goes beyond wisdom. It has to do with intuition; understanding timing and tone with insight into particulars; reading between the lines of what is being said and not being said; interpreting the meaning behind a given situation; and perceiving the unspoken reasons for people's actions. Although knowledge, wisdom, and discernment are not the same, they are all gifts from God. One need not be a Christian to have knowledge or wisdom; likewise, it is possible to be a Christian with inadequate knowledge and wisdom.

---

10. Dietrich Bonhoeffer, *Life Together* (New York: Harper & Row, 1954), 87.

But I am coming to believe that real discernment only comes from the Holy Spirit to those who are in right relationship with God.

King Solomon is known for being one of the wisest people to have ever lived. He is famous for his prayer asking for wisdom: "So give your servant a discerning heart to govern your people and to distinguish between right and wrong. For who is able to govern this great people of yours?" (1 Kings 3:9). Two important words from this prayer are "discerning" (*šō·mê·a'*) and "heart" (*lêḇ*). "Discerning" means to obey by hearing. The term "heart" in Hebrew does not refer to the organ that pumps blood; rather, it is the place of judgment and volition, or what we might refer to as the seat of understanding (the NRSV translates *lêḇ* in verse 9 as "an understanding mind").[11] When one seeks to obey God, one asks for a hearing heart that will be tender and sensitive to the voice of God. From this hearing comes a greater understanding and the potential of coming to God's point of view.

Solomon is given wisdom from God, but he never fully develops the hearing heart that he prays for. His decisions regarding foreign wives, international alliances, wealth-building, and idolatry make clear that he eventually stops listening.[12] Solomon has knowledge, but he cannot be our ultimate model for wisdom and discernment. Solomon's initial desires do not match his eventual obedience; wisdom does not grow into discernment.

We must have knowledge, wisdom, *and* discernment. Pastors do not have the luxury of omitting any of the three. I pray often for a listening heart that includes petitions for purity ("to will one thing"), humility ("to know where my strength comes from"), and wisdom

---

11. Karen Strand Winslow, *1 and 2 Kings: A Commentary in the Wesleyan Tradition*, New Beacon Bible Commentary (Kansas City, MO: Beacon Hill Press of Kansas City, 2017), 68.

12. "By the end of Solomon's story, he had become an anti-model of wisdom. He did not use his God-given wisdom to govern himself." Winslow, *1 and 2 Kings*, 109–10.

("to have the mind of Christ"). Seminaries can teach knowledge, but I have yet to find a class on wisdom and discernment. Wisdom and discernment only come by nurturing a hearing heart.

Many pastors are intellectually smart and knowledgeable but lack emotional and spiritual discernment and hard-earned, mature wisdom. Their ministries suffer because of it. We need knowledge and "depth of insight" (Philippians 1:9); renewed minds so we may "discern what is the will of God—what is good and acceptable and perfect" (Romans 12:2, NRSV). Intercession is one way that God gives pastors listening hearts, and that leads to the gift of discernment.

Have you ever had a true intercessor? A person who is committed to standing in the gap for you?

When I came to be the lead pastor at Bethany First Church of the Nazarene, Glaphré Gilliland became a cherished intercessor for me. Glaphré (pronounced GLAY-free) was the oldest child of one of my pastoral predecessors, Ponder Gilliland. She was single all her life and became a high school drama teacher. She also had a debilitating disease that eventually made her unable to leave her house. That was her condition when I came to be her pastor. But Glaphré was also known for her deep intimacy with Jesus. She was renowned throughout the evangelical world for her writings on prayer, and she taught thousands through a prayer ministry called Prayerlife.[13] When she asked if she could be one of my intercessors, I gladly said yes. Even though she passed only a short time later (almost exactly one year), those several months deeply impacted my life. We agreed that she would call me about twice a month to share what God was revealing to her through her intercession. I had a standing agreement with my assistant: "It doesn't matter if I'm in a meeting with the state governor—if Glaphré calls, come get me."

---

13. I often recommend her book, *When the Pieces Don't Fit*, as an inspirational guide to those wanting to nurture a listening heart for God. It remains one of the finest memoirs of personal faith and obedience to Christ that I have ever read.

The calls from her would proceed accordingly: "Pastor David, this is Glaph. I've been talking to the Lord about you all night long" (*all night?*). "This is what I am hearing." She would then tell me what the Holy Spirit had impressed upon her. Sometimes it was a scripture, or a phrase, or even a single word. But without exception, her messages from God would directly address, with eerie precision, a person or a situation I was currently dealing with. She didn't know the details *per se*, but she perceived the concepts. How could she have known? I hadn't told her about those things—but she knew. Did she have a hidden listening device in my office? Was she tapping my phone? No—she had gained the gift of discernment through intercession.[14] And the more she became aware in her spirit, the more intensely she prayed.

Another spiritual mentor of mine, Oswald Chambers, alludes to the mystery of discernment in intercession: "One of the most subtle and illusive burdens God ever places on us as his saints is this burden of discernment concerning others. He gives us discernment so that we may accept the responsibility for those souls before him and form the mind of Christ about them."[15] I am usually skeptical of strangers who walk into the church office and say, "Pastor, God told me to tell you to do this." They haven't personally invested in my life or earned the right to speak so directly from God. But Glaphré earned that right by lingering in the presence of God on my behalf. Chambers comments further, "It is not that we are able to bring God into contact with our minds, but that we awaken ourselves to the point where

---

14. Glaphré was a teacher to many people. A mutual friend once said to me, "Glaphré told me if I didn't have a secret with God, then I probably wasn't spending enough time with him. I've found that to be so true for me. She was an amazing teacher, and I'm still so grateful I was blessed to have her speak into my life. I believe prayer is hearing the heartbeat of God. I've always been good at talking to God, but it's in the listening and being still that I see him and hear his whispers."

15. Chambers, *My Utmost*, March 31, https://utmost.org/heedfulness-or-hypocrisy-in-ourselves/.

God is able to convey his mind to us regarding the people for whom we intercede."[16] I am convinced that is what God did for Glaphré. I am still amazed by how much she seemed to know about me (if you don't want someone to know you well, don't ask them to be an intercessor!). I am eternally grateful for the year of prayer that covered the beginning of my pastorate there.

The power of intercession also provides *protection*. The protection aspect works in two ways: a kind of covering for those who are being prayed for (Matthew 6:13) and a growing self-awareness of potential pitfalls to the beneficiary of intercession.

I vividly recall a conversation with JoAnne, another faithful intercessor in my second church. "Pastor David," she said, "I want you to know that I am praying daily for God to protect you from sexual temptation." I gave her my best pastoral smile and thanked her for her prayers, but I confess that inwardly I was rolling my eyes. My relationship with my wife, Christi, was strong, and our marriage was healthy. I didn't see the point of JoAnne's intercession for a problem that didn't exist.

A few days later the Lord checked me for that attitude: "David, who do you think you are? Do you think one of the reasons that isn't currently a temptation for you is that someone named JoAnne is praying that it won't be?" I realized that JoAnne's prayers of intercession provided protection when I wasn't even aware of my need for it, and they brought me a new attentiveness to latent danger.

I had to go back to JoAnne and apologize: "I'm sorry that I didn't take your prayers seriously before. I really believe your prayers are helping me. Please don't stop praying for my protection."

---

16. Chambers, *My Utmost*, March 31, https://utmost.org/heedfulness-or-hypocrisy-in-ourselves/.

It is true that "when we pray we give God a chance to work in the unconscious realm of the lives of those for whom we pray."[17] The result is spiritual alertness and preparation for tests and temptations.

Jesus as Intercessor

I close this chapter on intercession with a final observation. The reason I know this is so important to God and the kingdom is that interceding is exactly what Jesus is doing right now. "It is Christ Jesus, who died, yes, who was raised, who is at the right hand of God, who indeed intercedes for us" (Romans 8:34, NRSV). The incarnated, crucified, risen, ascended, and coming-again Christ is interceding for us and for the world he loves. John Ortberg puts it this way: "His teaching ministry lasted three years. His intercessory ministry has been going on for two thousand."[18] If the Son of God believes that intercession is that consequential, then sign me up.

"O Jerusalem, I have posted watchmen on your walls; they will pray day and night, continually. Take no rest, all you who pray to the LORD. Give the LORD no rest until he completes his work, until he makes Jerusalem the pride of the earth" (Isaiah 62:6–7, NLT).

---

17. Chambers, *Studies in the Sermon on the Mount*, 50.
18. Ortberg, *The Life You've Always Wanted*, 94.

INTERCESSION: HOW IT WORKS

The Bible's teaching on prayer—through prose and poetry, parables and storytelling—leads to an overwhelming conclusion: God takes the prayers of his people seriously. The biblical personalities from Abraham to John the Revelator prayed as if their prayers could and would make a difference. They believed that their prayers were heard, that their prayers mattered to God, and that, in some mysterious way, their prayers worked in a divine-human partnership to alter the course of the world.

In the last chapter, we considered the meaning, nature, and benefits of intercession. Now we come to the all-important matter of application. What does the practice of intercession look like for a praying pastor?

Practicing Intercession

There are so many things to pray about for a pastor. Regardless of the size of one's congregation, the needs that are represented can be overwhelming. Where does a pastor begin?

In his classic book on Christian community, written during the period when he led an underground seminary in Nazi Germany, Lutheran minister Dietrich Bonhoeffer expresses this need to his fellow pastors: "It is impossible to mention in the intercessions of corporate worship all the persons who are committed to our care, or at any rate to do so in the way that is required of us [in the day alone]."[1] It is reassuring to know that, even for one of the greatest theological minds and model shepherds of the last century, the intercession list felt long and unwieldy.

There are four ways the practice of intercession has become focused in my own life. I am not suggesting these become the sole focus of your journey of intercessory prayer. The Holy Spirit is faithful to shape our praying lives uniquely, in ways that fit us best. I only share them as a starting point.

1. Begin with Those You Live with and Know Best

If you're married, intercession starts with your spouse. Though never married himself (he was engaged to be married to Maria von Wedemeyer when he was executed), Bonhoeffer explained why this is true for every Christian: "Every Christian has his [sic] own circle who have requested him to make intercession for them or for whom he knows he has been called upon especially to pray. These will be, first of all, those with whom he must live day by day."[2] Christian wedding vows include exclusive rights and privileges that are physical, emotional, and spiritual. When we pray with and for our spouses, we know better how to serve them, they feel protected and loved, and intimacy increases. The first priority of intercessory prayer, for those who are married, is your husband or wife. In addition, if you have children or grandchildren, it is your privilege and responsibility to pray for them by name and circumstance.

I was blessed to be the beneficiary of praying parents. Hearing my dad pray for me every morning was profoundly impactful. I re-

---

1. Bonhoeffer, *Life Together*, 85.
2. Bonhoeffer, *Life Together*, 85.

member when the Lord impressed the same conviction upon me as a young father. After all, who knew the needs of my children better than me? Moreover, whom did I expect to carry the daily burden of prayer for them? Was it the job of their children's pastor? Or their Sunday school teacher? As I prayed for my kids, I became more aware of their spiritual and emotional needs, as the Holy Spirit gave me insight into better ways to guide and help them. I am persuaded that I knew specific and detailed things about them that I couldn't have known any other way but through intercessory prayer. Evidently, God had a way to know our children before we could spy on their social media profiles. That has not changed since they became adults. While I have been far from a perfect father, my kids and now grandkids know that, as long as I have breath in my lungs, there will be one person in the world who will be lifting their names and life situations every day to their heavenly Father. It is my promise to them.

I often take the opportunity to pray Scripture over my children and grandchildren. For example, "I pray that [Megan], being rooted and established in love, may have power, together with all the Lord's holy people, to grasp how wide and long and high and deep is the love of Christ, and to know this love that surpasses knowledge—that [Megan] may be filled to the measure of all the fullness of God" (Ephesians 3:17b–19).

Or for my college-age grandson, "[I pray that Jackson will] not conform to the pattern of this world, but [Jackson will] be transformed by the renewing of [Jackson's] mind. Then [Jackson] will be able to test and approve what God's will is—his good, pleasing and perfect will" (Romans 12:2).

Some of our most challenging intercession comes when praying for wandering or rebellious children. Prayer for prodigals comes naturally because the burden for them is heavy. Yet knowing how to pray for them can be difficult when we do not see changes. It is easy to explain to God how he should be helping them.

In a letter written to Philip Yancey, a mother of college-age students confessed, "I'm trying to pray less 'parentally,' in other words, telling God what to do. Rather, I try to look behind the symptoms of rebellion or risky behavior and ask God to help my children find better ways of finding meaning and of handling the stress in their lives."[3]

A friend of our family once told me: "The long journey with our daughter has been fraught with lots of emotional pain. After years of praying for her, I finally felt like I had run out of words to say to God. When I sensed anxiety rising in me, I found myself whispering a simple prayer, 'Lord, you know.' That three-word prayer is what got me through the toughest times." Intercession can be as easy as visualizing a face we love and saying, "Lord, you know." There have been times in my own life when my expectation for what I thought *should* happen caused me to miss something that actually *was* happening. I am learning to trust God to act *how* and *when* God sees fit. After all, he knows and loves my children even more than I do.

Even for a pastor who is committed to praying for many people and innumerable needs, your first priority in prayer is to your family. We should not feel guilty for making them our main concern.

2. Pray for Colleagues and Ministry Partners

The second group I pray for are colleagues and ministry partners. These are the people outside your household in closest proximity to you on a regular basis. These companions and coworkers, including pastoral staff and church board members, have been providentially placed in your life for the ministry season where you currently find yourself. You may not be able to pray every day for all the members of your church, but you can intercede for those in the next level of your concentric circle of relationships. The next level for

---

3. Yancey, *Prayer*, 60.

you may be Sunday school teachers, fellow elders, or church-adopted missionaries.

I often pray for my colleagues on the Church of the Nazarene's Board of General Superintendents, including their spouses and children, by name and situation. They are the ones who are currently in my closest sphere of influence and circle of relationships. I am in contact with them almost every day. We consult, deliberate, pray, laugh, and sometimes cry together. They are more than colleagues—they have become my friends. I also pray for various jurisdictional partners in ministry, senior leadership team members, and close friends. They are the faces God brings to my mind in prayer because I work with them so directly.

Prayers for our closest working associates may not spring from feelings of close attachment. Because someone is familiar doesn't mean we have a warm and fuzzy connection with them. Some of our working relationships are because of personal affinity and things we share in common (they are chosen). Other working relationships are because of elections and positions—people we would not have chosen if it were only up to us. They may not be enemies, but they aren't buddies either. Thankfully, intercession can be sincere without being overly dependent on affectionate feelings. Indeed, intercessory prayer protects communities of faith and allows for a gracious buffer with those who are different than us. It is exceedingly difficult to pray for someone and hold on to angry feelings toward them. Intercession for troubling relationships banishes bitterness. I know of no one who articulates this better than Bonhoeffer when he writes:

A Christian fellowship lives and exists by the intercession of its members for one another, or it collapses. I can no longer condemn or hate a brother [or sister] for whom I pray, no matter how much trouble they cause me. His [or her] face, that hitherto may have been strange and intolerable to me, is transformed in intercession into the countenance of a brother [or sister] for whom Christ died, the face of a forgiven sinner. That is a happy discovery for the Christian who begins to pray for others. There is no dislike, no personal tension, no estrangement that cannot be overcome by intercession as far as our side of it is concerned. Intercessory prayer is the purifying bath into which the individual and the fellowship must enter every day.[4]

How would our work look different if we became intercessors who stand in the gap for our closest colleagues and ministry partners? How would trust and honesty increase if we learned to pray in these ways? And not just in generalities, but specific and pondered—because interceding is loving, and loving is interceding. It can be as cleansing and refreshing to your faith community as a purifying bath.

3. Pray for What Is Most Important to You

This may seem like an odd and subjective way to pray. *Isn't this self-centered? And what if my passions are out of whack?* It all depends on what you believe about desire. Psalm 37:4 says, "Take delight in the LORD, and he will give you the desires of your heart." Does this mean that, when we devote our lives to God, he will give us what we want (or think we want)? A good job, a spouse, a loving marriage, a fulfilling career, prosperity? It seems obvious that is not what this verse is promising. Rather, when we are fully surrendered to God, the very desires that well up in us, even our deepest yearnings, are ordered and placed there by God. He gives us *his* desires, which then become the desires of *our* hearts. The things we love, the passions that emerge, what we most deeply desire are derived from the heart of God for us. Thus, when we pray according to the Spirit of God in us, we find our wills, dispositions, and the habituations of our hearts aligning with Father, Son, and Holy Spirit. We receive the mind of Christ, even for our highest aspirations. One could even say that "prayer makes it safe for God to give us many of the things we most desire."[5]

---

4. Bonhoeffer, *Life Together*, 86.

5. Keller, *Prayer*, 18.

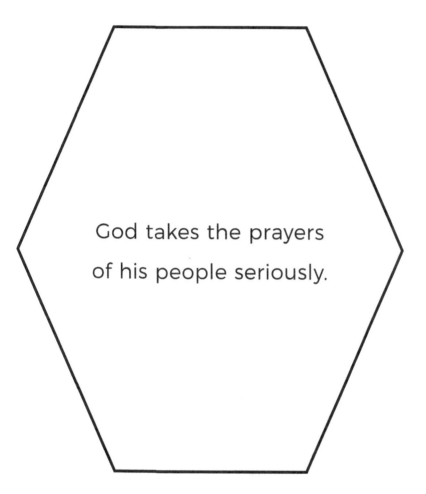

God takes the prayers of his people seriously.

I discovered this in my own call to ministry. The fact that I *wanted* to be a preacher was concerning to me. I had been led to believe that, when someone *wanted* to be in ministry, it was a sure sign they were calling themselves. I vaguely remember one sermon where the preacher declared in a high-pitched voice, "God has to bend you over a broken rail, looking straight into hell itself, before you know you have been appointed to preach the gospel!" I was only a teenager at the time and was not yet fully grappling with my life's calling, but the criterion seemed intense enough that I was pretty sure it hadn't happened to me. For that reason, when my desires began to lean in the direction of pastoral ministry, I needed confirmation from Psalm 37 that any longing to glorify God through my life came not from self-interest or the Enemy—but from the Lord, who put them there.

Have you ever known someone who was so laser-focused on a particular issue that you knew it was bound to come up in every conversation with them? Human trafficking or immigration or foster care might be important issues to you as well, but for that person, they have become passions. It's all they can talk about. Where did their passion come from? I believe that, if they are surrendered to Jesus Christ, it's likely it has been given to them from the Lord. It has become a desire of their heart.

Praying for those desires is as natural as breathing. You don't have to be forced to pray about what is most important to you. In fact, the opposite may be true. Dallas Willard makes the astute observation that "prayer simply dies from efforts to pray about 'good things' that honestly do not matter to us."[6] Things only begin to matter to us when they become the desires of our hearts. It should be apparent that this does not give license for prayer to become introverted and myopic, focused only on our needs and the needs of those closest to

---

6. Dallas Willard, *The Divine Conspiracy: Rediscovering Our Hidden Life in God* (New York: HarperCollins, 1998), 242.

us.[7] God is our Father, not our butler. On the other hand, praying for what is most important to us is never condemned in Scripture. Willard continues, "Many people have found prayer impossible because they thought they should only pray for wonderful but remote needs they actually had little or no interest in or even knowledge of. . . . The way to get to meaningful prayer for those good things is to start praying for what we are truly interested in. The circle of our interests will inevitably grow in the largeness of God's love."[8]

Growing up in the church and being raised in a strong Christian family does not guarantee that a child will have faith. My childhood and early teen years were fairly sheltered, and I considered myself to be a Christian most of that time. However, during my late high school and early college years, I drifted away from God and, as a result, began distancing myself from the church. (There was an entire year when I attended church only once—to get married.) I became a prodigal son of my home church. Many folks were worried about me, including my parents, pastors, and friends.

What I didn't know at the time was that there was a group of four men in the church who knew me and loved me. They carried such a burden for me that they committed to meet together at the church every Wednesday morning for the express purpose of "praying for David Busic's salvation." They didn't spend those Wednesdays praying about world affairs, social reforms, church conflicts, or political divides. They prayed for *me*—exclusively and specifically, and for a long time. It was one of the most miserable years of my life! (Holy Spirit conviction is usually not intended for our happiness.) But it was also one of the best years of my life because my heart was changed. Only after a renewed consecration of my life to God and a

---

7. Al Truesdale, *When You Can't Pray: Finding Hope When You're Not Experiencing God*, 2nd ed. (Kansas City, MO: Beacon Hill Press of Kansas City, 2016), 79.

8. Willard, *The Divine Conspiracy*, 242.

return to church did I even learn they had been praying. I'm so glad they did; I am indebted to them for their care. Like the four friends (intercessors) who moved heaven and earth to bring a paralyzed man to Jesus, these four intercessors stood in the gap for me because God had made me the desire of their hearts. "When Jesus saw *their* faith" (Mark 2:5), sins were forgiven and bodies restored.

It bears repeating: interceding is loving, and loving is interceding. The opposite of love is not hate; it is indifference.

4. Pay Attention to Divine Appointments

I am occasionally asked, "As a general superintendent responsible for so many, how do you intercede for the church around the world?" To say that the needs are vast is an understatement. I would be less than truthful if I told you I prayed for every country, missionary, local church, and pastor regularly. But I have learned to be okay with that because of a fundamental but deeply held certainty: *God orders my steps.* By this, I do not mean that I advocate for determinism in any sense, or that my free will is not a factor and that my obedience or disobedience to God doesn't matter. I am morally responsible for my actions, and not everything that happens is preordained. I need not pray before lunch over which chicken restaurant I should patronize. ("Lord, will it be KFC or Chick-fil-A?")

Having said that, neither am I an agnostic who believes God has better things to do than play chess with our lives and coordinate divine appointments. Nor am I a deist, believing that God created a mechanistic universe but has decided to distance himself and doesn't give much attention to the daily stuff of life. If Jesus stresses that the Father is interested in such things as the number of hairs on our head and sparrows that fall to the ground (Matthew 10:29–30), then surely the details of our lives matter and are accounted for in the providence of God.

Scripture offers strong support for ongoing guidance and direction in a believer's life. It is not the exception; it is the rule.

*The LORD directs the steps of the godly. He delights in every detail
of their lives.
(Psalm 37:23, NLT)*

*Teach me to do your will, for you are my God; may your good
Spirit lead me on level ground.
(Psalm 143:10)*

*Then you will call, and the LORD will answer; you will cry for
help, and he will say: Here am I.
The LORD will guide you always.
(Isaiah 58:9, 11a)*

*The human mind plans the way, but the LORD directs the steps.
(Proverbs 16:9, NRSV)*

*This what the LORD says—your Redeemer, the Holy One of Israel:
"I am the LORD your God, who teaches you what is good for you
and leads you along the paths you should follow."
(Isaiah 48:17, NLT)*

*Since we are living by the Spirit, let us follow the Spirit's leading
in every part of our lives.
(Galatians 5:25, NLT)*

These biblical witnesses, and many like them, seem to say that hearing from God is needed and expected. Guidance is assumed, and for guidance to be necessary, it makes sense to believe that our lives are not random but ordered in a purposeful and sustained way. For those who get nervous that something akin to listening to the voice of God will lead to irrational fanaticism and absurd recklessness, imagine the alternative: a life lived without the providential care and clear guidance of a higher power. Willard's point is spot on: "Isn't it more presumptuous and dangerous, in fact, to undertake human existence *without* hearing God?"[9] Indeed, the saints of the ages have regarded personal communion with God as communication that is like daily manna—given afresh every day as a gift.

As a general rule, we are in God's will whenever we are following Jesus. That is, by definition, the meaning of discipleship. "The answering word," Frederick Buechner rightly says, comes "only after the [listening] word."[10] But it doesn't take away the fact that the reason we must have daily guidance from God is that God's very guidance "leaves a lot of room for initiative on our part, which is essential: our individual initiatives are central to his will for us."[11] Said differently, how we respond to God's leading is essential. God guides, but we follow. God invites, but we take the initiative. God empowers, but we act. He will not do that for us.

Isaiah entered worship in the temple to make sacrifices to God. He heard the voice of the Lord make a general invitation: "Whom shall I send? And who will go for us?" Isaiah stepped up, "Here am I. Send me!" (Isaiah 6:8).

Jesus entered a synagogue where there was a man with a withered hand (Mark 3:1–6). Jesus invited the man to come to him and told him to stretch out his hand. When he did, his hand was completely restored. Jesus invited, but the man had to act. Jesus did not stretch out the man's hand for him. God will not do for us what we must do for ourselves. In almost every case, human freedom and initiative are required.

Acts 8–10 is a biblical case study of how this works (Philip and the Ethiopian eunuch; Saul/Paul and Ananias; Peter and Cornelius). In each case, God arranged surprisingly detailed intersections of

---

9. Willard, *Hearing God: Developing a Conversational Relationship with God* (Downers Grove, IL: InterVarsity Press, 2012), 9.

10. Frederick Buechner, *Telling the Truth: The Gospel as Tragedy, Comedy, and Fairy Tale* (New York: Harper and Row, 1977), 35. Quoted in Truesdale, *When You Can't Pray*, 33.

11. Willard, *Hearing God*, 11.

both the messengers and the receivers; ambassadors and recipients. God invited—they initiated. God spoke—they acted. The results were perfectly ordered, impeccably timed, Spirit-led encounters that shaped salvation history. No wonder, then, that Paul would later write to the Galatian Christians, "Since we live by the Spirit, let us keep in step with the Spirit" (Galatians 5:25).

When we believe that God orders our steps, we discover that every day is full of open doors and opportunities. God has plans that include us. Divinely appointed intersections await. The problem isn't on God's side—it's *our* lack of perception. We just don't notice.

What if each person we meet on a given day is not by chance? What if these run-ins are not by accident or coincidence? The server at your restaurant; the cashier at the grocery store; the neighbor who jogs by your house every morning; the postal worker who waves at you when they drop off your mail. The appointments, the meetings, the phone calls, the emails, the surprises, the interruptions, the so-called ordinary interactions that fill up every day—what if all of these are invitations to prayer? What if part of intercessory prayer is paying attention to the seemingly routine details and allowing the Holy Spirit to teach us to pray without ceasing? What if these are opportunities to bless, encourage, and lift up weary, lonely, searching people in Jesus's name (even under the cover of silent prayer)? Such was the belief of Oswald Chambers: "The circumstances of a saint's life are ordained of God. In the life of a saint there is no such thing as chance. God by his providence brings you into circumstances that you can't understand at all, but the Spirit of God understands. God brings you to places, among people, and into certain conditions to accomplish a definite purpose through the intercession of the Spirit in you."[12]

We need not know a person's name or the details of their situation. The Holy Spirit makes us sensitive to their needs. If we can see

---

12. Chambers, *My Utmost*, November 7, https://utmost.org/the-undetected -sacredness-of-circumstances/.

If every Christian
alive today
would only be
faithful to pray for daily
promptings from the Holy
Spirit, and for those people in
their circle of relationships
and spheres of influence,
intercessory prayer
would cover the
entire world 24/7.

their face, we can love them enough to pray for them. C. S. Lewis made it a spiritual practice to pray for his daily encounters: "I am afraid many people appear in my prayers only as 'that old man at Crewe' or 'the waitress' or even 'that man.' One may have lost, or may never have known their names and yet remember how badly they needed to be prayed for."[13]

This has become part of my daily intercession. I pray over the encounters and conversations of the day as the Lord brings them to my mind. I bear the responsibility for these interactions because my steps have been so ordered by God. (Oswald Chambers refers to them as "the undetected sacredness of circumstances.")[14]

It should not surprise us that divine appointments happen most often in our own neighborhoods and workplaces. A few years ago, I was at McCall Lake in Idaho, spending a week with close friends. On an evening walk, one of my retired pastor friends said to me, "David, nudges are important—those small, almost imperceptible prompts from the Holy Spirit. I have learned to pay attention to those guiding nudges: the nudge of warning, the nudge of evangelism, the nudge of wisdom." His insight resonated with my experience. I had never heard them referred to as nudges before, but I have come to associate the term with the still, small voice. Tod Bolsinger explains, "It's not audible as much as an impression, but I have learned to listen very closely."[15]

My colleague and friend, General Superintendent Emeritus Jim Diehl, once told me, "Never forget that the Holy Spirit speaks through checks and prompts. Checks," he said, "are red lights in

---

13. Lewis, *Letters to Malcolm*, 18–19. Lewis jokingly alludes to times when he cannot remember the names of people brought to his mind to pray for: "why you find it so important to pray for people by their Christian names I can't imagine. I always assume God knows their surnames as well."

14. Chambers, *My Utmost*, November 7, https://utmost.org/the-undetected -sacredness-of-circumstances/.

15. Tod Bolsinger, *Canoeing the Mountains: Christian Leadership in Uncharted Territory* (Downers Grove, IL: InterVarsity Press, 2015), 36.

your spirit." Checks can be: *stop; watch; listen; be careful; don't say that; change directions.* Checks can also bring to mind a bad attitude or un-Christlike spirit, and can help us know who can be trusted and who cannot. "Prompts," Diehl continued, "are green lights." Prompts can be: *go; act; move; speak up; say this; do that; encourage her; make a phone call; check on his family; love.* In this manner, according to Jim, the Holy Spirit continually guides the fully consecrated person. He orders our steps with checks and prompts, and as we walk in the light we have been given, the Spirit opens others to the gospel message.

A fascinating example of how checks and prompts work in the lives of individuals and communities of faith is found in Acts 16.[16] Paul and Silas are traveling through the area of Phrygia and Galatia (modern-day Turkey) on a missionary tour. That was not their initial plan. Their original destination was in another part of Asia Minor, but they are diverted—not by the weather or a bad map—but because they are "kept by the Holy Spirit from preaching the word in the province of Asia" (v. 6). Then, upon coming to the borders of Mysia, they head north for the province of Bithynia, but again, "the Spirit of Jesus would not allow them to" (v. 7), forcing them to take yet another route. Because Paul and Silas don't kick down the closed doors, Paul is given a vision in the night of a man from Macedonia pleading for them to come and help. Confident that this is the direction they have been seeking, they "*immediately* tried to cross over to Macedonia, being convinced that God had called us to proclaim the good news to them" (v. 10, NRSV, emphasis added). No doubt, this entire process is immersed in a great deal of prayer for guidance and clarity. Much discernment is needed, including constant interpretation of what the Spirit is saying. However, through various twists and turns, these Spir-

---

16. After Pentecost, we never read again of the early church casting lots as a practice for discerning God's will (Acts 1:26). Guidance comes thereafter from the indwelling Holy Spirit.

it-filled, Spirit-led missionaries are directed down a path that eventually takes them to Philippi, and the rest is salvation history.

Notice the checks and prompts that lead to eventual openness to the gospel:

- Acts 16:6 (check): "kept by the Holy Spirit from preaching the word in the province of Asia."
- Acts 16:7 (check): "the Spirit of Jesus would not allow them to."
- Acts 16:9 (prompt): "during the night Paul had a vision."
- Acts 16:13 (prompt): "on the Sabbath we went outside the city gate to the river."
- Acts 16:14 (open hearts): "the Lord opened her heart."

A Trappist monk once said, "God gets us where He wants us, no matter the machinations."[17] Oswald Chambers often says the Holy Spirit guides us through the engineering of our circumstances. Sometimes doors open (green lights); sometimes doors close (red lights). Plots and schemes abound. Disappointments often become breakthroughs. Nevertheless, by any means necessary ("by hook or by crook"), we can trust that, when we don't ignore the nudges and pay close attention to the still, small voice, we will eventually get to Philippi.

In Step with the Spirit

I have had experiences of driving down the road, noticing a person in the car next to me, and thinking, *That looks like my friend Sam.* It's not Sam, but now Sam is on my mind, and I can't quit thinking about him: *I wonder how Sam's doing? The last time I talked to him he was in a job transition. I hope everything turned out for the best.* The longer I think about Sam, the more I feel led by the Holy Spirit

---

17. J. D. Walt, "When the Door Closes (Or Gets Slammed in Your Face), *Seedbed Daily Text*, September 3, 2019, https://www.seedbed.com/door-closes-gets-slammed-face/.

to pray for him. Is that a coincidence?[18] Did Sam randomly pop into my mind out of the deep recesses of my brain's gray matter? Or is it more than that? Are these sorts of impressions Spirit-directed? A prompt to intercede?

I was having breakfast at a hotel in Maputo, Mozambique. Seemingly out of the blue, a pastor friend's face popped into my brain. He is a well-regarded and faithful pastor who has led the same urban congregation for more than twenty years. Yet I hadn't thought about him for a long time. Why now, while eating an omelet? I couldn't get him off my mind. I sensed it was the still, small voice. Though I was ten hours ahead in time zones, I took a chance and texted him to let him know I was thinking about him and praying for him. In just a few minutes he replied: "So good to hear from you. I can't believe your timing! This has been one of the most challenging seasons of my ministry. Even now, I am putting words to paper on what I need to say to my church tomorrow morning. Thank you for the reminder that the Lord is with me." I'm so thankful I didn't ignore the impression to pray and reach out. Though more than 10,000 miles (17,000 kilometers) away, it felt like a divine appointment.

How do I know an impression is from the Spirit? There are three questions I ask myself to determine if what I am sensing is from the Lord, or an overladen sense of duty, a guilt-ridden conscience, or just indigestion.

1. Is It Scriptural?

If what I feel impressed to do violates the Word of God, I can be assured it is not from the Lord. It is preposterous to think that God would ask me to do anything that is contrary to his written Word. What is easily rationalized in a moment is exposed by the truth.

---

18. William Temple famously said, "All I know is that when I pray coincidences happen, and when I don't pray they don't happen." I also read somewhere, "A coincidence for the Christian is God undercover."

2. Is It Self-Promoting?

Sometimes we can do the right thing for the wrong reason. Do I feel led to do this thing because I want the person to think I'm a good pastor? Am I feeling prompted to do this for the sake of my image and what others think of me? Do I want to defend myself and give someone my side of the story? I have discovered that, when my motivation is self-oriented, self-protective, or self-promoting, either the idea is wrong or the timing is off.

3. Is It Persistent?

If something is from the Lord, it usually won't go away. In fact, every time I pray, it tends to grow in its largeness. The longer I listen and obey, the brighter and clearer the light becomes illuminating what I need to do (1 John 1:5–7). Ever-increasing awareness in prayer regarding a person or situation is usually a sign for me that it is the Lord speaking.

I am coming to believe that when we don't hear perfectly—or even when we get it wrong—if it's done out of a heart of love and humility, with our only motive to glorify God, our good Father has mercy on us, even blessing our attempts. "If we pray—even if in wrong ways," Richard Foster writes, "God is pleased with our feeble efforts and Jesus lovingly guides us into more excellent ways."[19] When these three questions are answered harmoniously, it is a good indication that the Spirit of God is directing you.

Faithful, Focused Prayer

These are four ways I focus my intercession as a praying leader. Much of it is about awareness and being alert to the God-happenings all around us. We learn to pray: *"God, open our eyes to see what you see, our minds to think what you think, our ears to hear what you hear,*

---

19. Richard Foster, *Devotional Classics* (New York: HarperCollins, 2005), 131.

and our hearts to desire what you desire." Pastor Paul urges the same to the believers under his care: "Pray in the Spirit at all times and on every occasion. Stay alert and be persistent in your prayers for all believers everywhere" (Ephesians 6:18, NLT).

Praying at all times with our eyes wide open could change the way we think about pastoral care and how we intercede for our congregations. It will require sensitivity to the Holy Spirit and a willingness to be a praying pastor. In the words of the fictional eleven-year-old musical prodigy in the movie *August Rush*, "The music is all around us. All you have to do—is listen."

I have a theory. If every Christian alive today would only be faithful to pray for daily promptings from the Holy Spirit, and for those people in their circle of relationships and spheres of influence, intercessory prayer would cover the entire world 24/7. The sun would never set on the blanket of righteous prayer.[20]

---

20. "Your part in intercessory prayer is not to agonize over how to intercede but to use the everyday circumstances and people God puts around you by his providence to bring them before his throne, and to allow the Spirit in you the opportunity to intercede for them. In this way God is going to touch the whole world with his saints." Chambers, *My Utmost*, November 7, https://utmost.org/the-undetected-sacredness-of-circumstances/.

AFTERWORD: WHERE DOES OUR HELP COME FROM?

I lift up my eyes to the mountains—
where does my help come from?
My help comes from the LORD,
the Maker of heaven and earth.

He will not let your foot slip—
he who watches over you will not slumber;
indeed, he who watches over Israel
will neither slumber nor sleep.

The LORD watches over you—
the LORD is your shade at your right hand;
the sun will not harm you by day,
nor the moon by night.

The LORD will keep you from all harm—
he will watch over your life;
the LORD will watch over your coming and going
both now and forevermore.
(Psalm 121)

Psalm 121 is one of my favorite psalms, especially as it pertains to church leadership. As you know, there are several different genres of psalms. Psalm 121 is a psalm of ascent, written to be sung as the Israelites made their annual trek to Jerusalem for the Festival of Passover.[1] Whole families came to worship God at the temple of Solomon. According to the Gospel writer Luke, Jesus's parents made this journey every year (2:41).

Jerusalem is located on a high mountain ridge. So, from whatever direction one approaches, that person is traveling through the mountainous region of the Judean hills. Most of the pilgrims would be coming from the north, and that road would be in hill country all the way. Eugene Peterson makes the valid point that in the first millennium BC, when a traveling Israelite lifted up their eyes to the hills surrounding Jerusalem, they would see a disturbing sight: Baal worship. Baal, the Canaanite god, was worshiped on the hilltops, so every hill that amounted to anything in Palestine had a shrine to Baal that was frequented by the local populace. And the worship was a particularly vile kind, centered around cult prostitution and involving self-inflicted wounds.[2]

It is a sad irony that Solomon was responsible for these "high places." The very person who built the temple to worship the one God also permitted the worship of local and foreign gods. This serves as a warning to pastors of the danger of ignoring or promoting syncretistic idolatry of any cultural kind or variety. Idolatry is whatever we need in addition to Jesus for our happiness, and it is widely practiced in subtle, even imperceptible ways. It's not that we don't want Jesus. It's that we want Jesus *plus*—Jesus *in addition to* oth-

---

1. Scholars agree that there are fifteen psalms designated as psalms of ascent (Psalms 120–134), each beginning with the Hebrew superscription "Song of Ascents." They have also been called pilgrim songs.

2. Eugene Peterson, *Every Step an Arrival* (Colorado Springs: Waterbrook, 2018), 125.

er things we lean on. Just like the Hebrews, who wanted to worship Yahweh in the temple *in addition to* Baal in the high places, we want to cover all our bases.

This is an acute temptation for pastors. An idol in the making is whatever we depend on except Jesus when we're in trouble, facing a crisis, or stress is high: "I lift up my eyes to (fill in the blank)."

I've taken the liberty of filling in a few blanks I've heard from some pastors lately, and even my own:

I lift up my eyes to life in the church the way it used to be.

I lift up my eyes to the time when the church was the center of cultural life [also known as Christendom].

I lift up my eyes to what I know best and am most comfortable with.

I lift up my eyes to this strategy, that method, or the newest book.

Do these sound familiar? You can fill in your own blank. And here's the thing: these things are not inherently bad. But they can't be our first *or* final go-to for help.

Psalm 121 is an antidote to any "lift up my eyes" solutions other than God. "I lift up my eyes to the mountains that are filled with other solutions *in addition to* Yahweh. But is this where my help comes from?" The psalmist answers with a definitive, "No! Our help comes from the LORD, who made heaven and earth—in fact, who made these very mountains! It all belongs to him. I can depend on this God—on *my* God."

As for me, I am done with cheap substitutes. I am done with prayerless striving in ministry. I want to be more than a pastor who prays. I want to be a praying pastor. The enormity of our task is too great for anything less.

I have not perfected the practice. I am still growing. I'm thankful for a heavenly Father who does not love me from a distance but who is exceedingly patient and persistent with me. I am learning to lead from my knees. And it feels, more and more, as though I am hearing what the Holy Spirit is saying to the church.

I leave you with a challenge. Pastor, don't play it safe this year. Pray dangerous, audacious prayers. Then act with holy courage and risk something great for the glory of God. Don't ask God for greener grass. Ask God to open your eyes to see what (or who) is right in front of you. Being a praying pastor will turn your theology into experience.[3]

By God's grace, it is possible. I am standing in the gap for you, even now.

---

3. Keller, *Prayer*, 80.